Storyscaping

Holistic Approaches to Improving the Skills of Story Writing

by
Bob Stanish

Featuring Artwork by Leonardo da Vinci

salubrious—
promoting health &
well-being
—good for the
soul —

Copyright © 1994, Good Apple

ISBN No. 0-86653-814-3

Printing No. 987654321

Good Apple
1204 Buchanan St., Box 299
Carthage, IL 62321-0299

Paramount Publishing

Dedication

This book is dedicated to the memory of my mom, Mary G. Stanish, and to her descendants and mine, Jon, Lin, and Brad. This book is also dedicated to the memory of my grandmother, Blanche Hake, an artist, who gave me a passionate love for art.

Leonardo da Vinci. *Study of a Tree*–Windsor, Royal Collection.

GA1506

Table of Contents

The Exercises

GA1506

The Appendix

Leonardo da Vinci. Windsor, Royal Collection.

GA1506

Introduction

Flexible Structuring Within Exercises

In my lifelong studies, investigations, and experimentations with written creative expression among students of various ages and abilities, I've found that flexible structuring can trigger some amazing results. In other words, as a teacher, if I set certain limitations or restraints or contingencies and perimeters to assignments that called for written narrative expression, and if I placed options or choices within those limitations, student-written products became vastly improved and, in many cases, professionally publishable. And in several cases they were.

This book contains the contingency or restraining elements I've used in classrooms to provide a flexible structure for student-written expression. To simply say to a group of students, "Write something interesting or creative about . . ." is ludicrous! As teachers, we need to provide a structure by which students can write.

In what ways might this be done? It can be done in several ways. A beginning of a story can be provided in which a conclusion is requested, or a conclusion can be provided in which a beginning is requested, or choices can be provided on a morphological matrix, or elements of a text can be provided in which the missing elements are requested. The exercises in this book contain all of the above and more.

Motivate Through Variety

There are many genres of writing. Why is it that we expect that just a few genres will appeal to all students? Some students are more motivated to write mysteries; some prefer satire; some prefer science fiction; and some prefer Gothic tales and stories. There are many varied ways to motivate students to write, and some of those varied ways are the varied genres themselves.

An effort has been made to provide a variety of genres in this book. There are very few teacher resource books that attempt to do this. One such book is the *ABC's of Creative Writing* (Booth and Skinner, 1981). This book provides a variety of genres, but student involvement is limited to responding to a set of provided questions.

Making Connections Among Genres

There are certain common elements that stories share, regardless of the type, kind, or category of story. Most stories deal with mood, characters, setting, plots or conflicts, and resolutions of those conflicts. We would expect to find the same elements in a folktale as we would a short story. So therefore, why not teach the elements of good writing through a variety of literary styles and works? In doing this, genres will find their suitors, that is, the students. One can teach the elements of grammar and style just as easily through a parody as one would with a vignette.

Structural Springboarding

By using flexible structuring within exercises and by using the exercises as learning motifs for varied genres, two purposes are served. One is the understanding that writing requires structure and the other is the recognition of and having experiences in a particular genre. This has a tendency, with practice and exposure, to motivate students to inaugurate their own independent ventures into writing just for the enjoyment and the intrinsic desire to do so. This has a springboard effect, that is, springboarding students from a provided structure to building their own structure. It is this kind of transfer that is the most important in any educational setting or instruction. This is the premise I've used in developing the skills of writing in my elementary, middle, and secondary school classrooms.

GA1506

Quirks and Their Reasons for Being

Humor and the use of humor are occasionally dispersed throughout this book. There are reasons for this. The most important reason is that originality is correlated with humor and originality is important in writing. Some of the format choices provided in Science Fiction Satire and A Western and other exercises are hilarious and are there to stimulate original thinking and additional humor. Another reason for humor is that I like humor. I believe there should be opportunities in a classroom to laugh, have fun, and to enjoy learning.

Another quirk is that rather than including a variety of previously published literary works on varied genres, I just decided to write them myself. In doing this, I could provide a more consistent format, insert humor whenever I felt like it, and provide myself with a never-ending challenge and a learning opportunity to understand more fully the breadth of what is defined as literature.

Writing as Thinking

Continuing with quirks, I placed on assignment the public domain of Leonardo da Vinci for illustrating this book. Da Vinci might have been the greatest thinker ever. Writing, I think, consists of thinking skills. I just thought Leonardo would do nicely. To fluently generate many story ideas for a potential story is a divergent thinking skill. To select one idea from a generated array of story ideas is a convergent thinking skill. Embellishing on an idea is elaboration which is another thinking skill and so are analysis, synthesis, prioritizing, comprehending, applying, classifying, sequencing, forecasting, hypothesizing, and evaluating. I've tried to structure within the format of this book provisions for these skills of thinking.

Writing as Holistic

Writing should be viewed as a holistic thing, for quality writing accentuates the importance of the whole. It is easy to get into intellectual quagmires on spelling, punctuation, and penmanship and lose sight of sequencing, continuity, and interest.

In viewing writing as holistic, stress the importance of the whole. Place as much importance on establishing an effective plot as punctuation or, for that matter, any other element of writing. Writing in itself is imperfect. Don't expect to find perfection. The original copy of Abraham Lincoln's Gettysburg Address is full of errors and so is almost every book that ever has been published. Take a red pen to any newspaper and mark the errors of fragmented sentences, spelling, and grammar. I'm not endorsing imperfection; it's just a fact of life in writing. Sometimes, as teachers, we place too much importance on the segmented parts of writing and not the whole.

Writing as Whole Language

In accepting writing as whole language, a wider universe is available. The lyrics of a song are as important as the persuasive language in an advertisement or any other genre including a novel. Words function in wondrous and varied ways. Writing is for everyone. That's why there are so many usages of writing in this book.

Writing as Play

There are opportunities in this book to play with words. And there should be opportunities to play with words in any classroom. The more we play with words and their meanings, the more analytical we become. The more we play with words and their meanings, the more meaningful we become in our capacities to express our thoughts and feelings. In the exercises Hundreds of Ways to See the World through Haiku, Hound Dawg and Po Possum, Turn on Dynamatron Rex! and Concrete Poetry, there are opportunities to play with words.

Writing as a Visual Mechanism

There is white space in this book and it's there for a reason. White space is that area of a page without words. In judiciously using white space on a printed page, there is a greater potential for comprehending what is said on that page. I've found, as a teacher and writer, that material containing white space is more

GA1506

inviting to a reader. This technique has been used for years with brochures and advertising material. When visual thinking combines with reading, it augments comprehension.

Writing as Ownership

This is, perhaps, one of the most important features of this book. The purpose for giving exercise titles to students (see the exercise pages) is that of ownership. I want them to own their completed work. I want them to feel pride and achievement in what they have written. Even though story excerpts are provided or formats are given to create stories, emphasize to students that they are the authors. The stories belong to them. If they wish to enter their stories in competitive contests or for publication purposes, there are no copyright infringements preventing them from doing so. This is not an endorsement for competitive contests, just a suggestion. I do endorse publications of student writings.

Teacher Stuff

Within this book are sections that attempt to accommodate expectations certain schools and states place on teachers. In the appendix section are objectives for each exercise. They will, assuredly, require some modification due to age and ability levels of students. Also in the appendix section is a list of words that are usable in phrasing classroom questions or for establishing daily lesson plan objectives or for writing units of instruction that require objectives. Also included are some sample test items. As with the objectives, modifications will be necessary.

Comments and Other Idiosyncrasies Throughout the Book

I have a compulsion to inundate certain pages of published print with personal feelings and thoughts about teaching, learning, education, and other things. It is not intended that everyone nor anyone should accept my thoughts or beliefs. They are just there because I'm me.

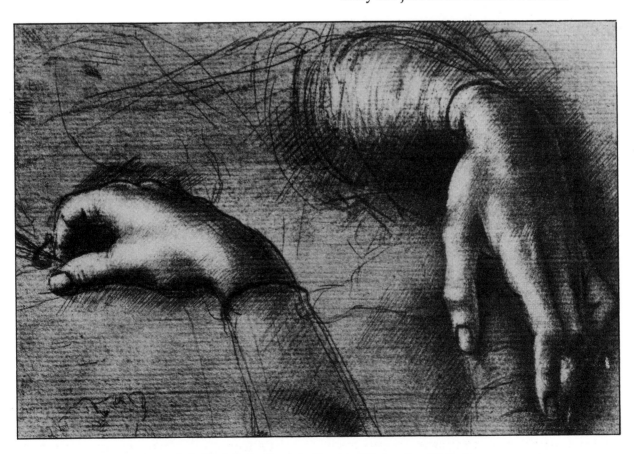

Leonardo da Vinci. *Study of hands for Mona Lisa*–Windsor, Royal Collection.

GA1506

The Storyscaping Genres

GA1506

"Of Course . . ."

Monologue: A speech given by one actor.

Mystery: A story that includes one or more of the following: suspense, espionage, detectives, crimes, or people pursued by some menace.

Fill in the blanks to make the partially done mystery complete. Make the mystery more humorous with your additions. When finished, read it to your classmates as a monologue.

"Of Course . . ."

by _____

Of course, it wasn't easy. And there were times I didn't know what to do. But I trusted my instincts. I always trust my instincts on these kinds of matters. There was something about Hubert that didn't make sense. Maybe it was his alibi or the way he dressed. I can recall what he wore at Penelope's party. He had on _____

_____

_____

_____

Strange I thought! But then, in my business you accept the strange and weird. And Hubert was definitely weird. He was impervious to stares when he was dunking for sliced pears in the fruit bowl. Penelope thought it was hilarious. I thought it was weird. I lost my appetite for the smorgasbord. The strangest thing of all was when he _____

_____

_____

_____

_____

_____

_____

_____

_____

_____

_____

_____

For information on the exercises refer to the Appendix.

"Of Course . . ."

by _____

Mrs. Gertrude Gimbal Grumble, after the fruit bowl incident, spoke to me. I was blinded by her baubles of sparkling blue diamonds that draped her neck. I reached for my sunglasses. I really couldn't stand the woman, but being polite, I listened to her idle babble about her expensive baubles. After her babbling, she said something about Penelope that I didn't know. "Penelope," she said, "was_____

_____

_____

_____

_____

_____

_____

_____

Hm, I thought.

It was 9:00 p.m. I always know the time because I look at my watch every thirty seconds. In my business, it's always important to know the time. The lights went out at 9:00 and that was followed, thirty seconds later, by a wretched and bloodcurdling scream. I reached for my pocket flashlight in my left breast pocket of my herringbone sport coat. In my business it's always important to be prepared for the unexpected. I quickly surveyed the ballroom, and on the floor by the fruit bowl was Mrs. Gertrude Gimbal Grumble. She had a dinner fork stuck in her, and her neck was bare of the baubles of sparkling blue diamonds.

I had to think and act fast to restore some order to the chaos. I immediately _____

_____

_____

_____

_____

_____

_____

_____

For information on the exercises refer to the Appendix.

GA1506

"Of Course . . ."

by _____

Of course, after having restored the lights and order, I asked for alibis. Hubert's excuse was the sizable quantity of fruit he had swallowed. He complained that severe stomach cramps prevented any movements on his part. Hm, I thought.

Penelope's alibi was that she _____

_____

_____

_____

_____

_____

_____

_____

_____

_____

_____

_____

Hm, I thought.

Well, as I said, I trust my instincts and my instincts told me that it had to be Hubert or Penelope or both. In addition to my instincts, there were only four people around the fruit bowl. There were the late Mrs. Gertrude Gimbal Grumble with her baubles of sparkling blue diamonds, Hubert, Penelope, and me. Of course, I didn't do it nor did the late Mrs. Gertrude Gimbal Grumble. So that leaves Hubert, Penelope, or both as the prime suspects.

Of course, the motive was obvious. It had to be the baubles of sparkling blue diamonds because they were missing. For awhile I thought the motive might have been her idle babble about her expensive baubles. Someone could have forked her just for the idle, lucid, ludicrous babble she babbled over her baubles. I mean, I sort of felt like doing it myself. But, of course, I didn't.

But this time I was really on my instincts and my instincts told me I was thirsty. I thought to heck with Hubert, and dipped a glass into the fruit bowl for some fruit juice. There at the bottom of the fruit bowl were the expensive baubles.

For information on the exercises refer to the Appendix.

"Of Course . . ."

by _____

Clever, I thought. No fingerprints. But then _____
ran from the room. Of course, my instincts told me to pursue. Which I did.

I _____

_____

_____

_____

_____

_____

_____

_____

_____

_____

_____

_____

_____

_____

_____

_____

_____

_____

_____

_____

_____

_____

Well, there you have it. Of course, it wasn't easy. These things never are. But I trusted my instincts. I always trust my instincts on these kinds of matters.

For information on the exercises refer to the Appendix.

GA1506

The origins of expressive language are based upon needs.
The need to express a feeling.
The need to express a thought.

[Stanish, 1990]

That's what this book is about.

Leonardo da Vinci. *Terraced house*–Codex Arundel

GA1506

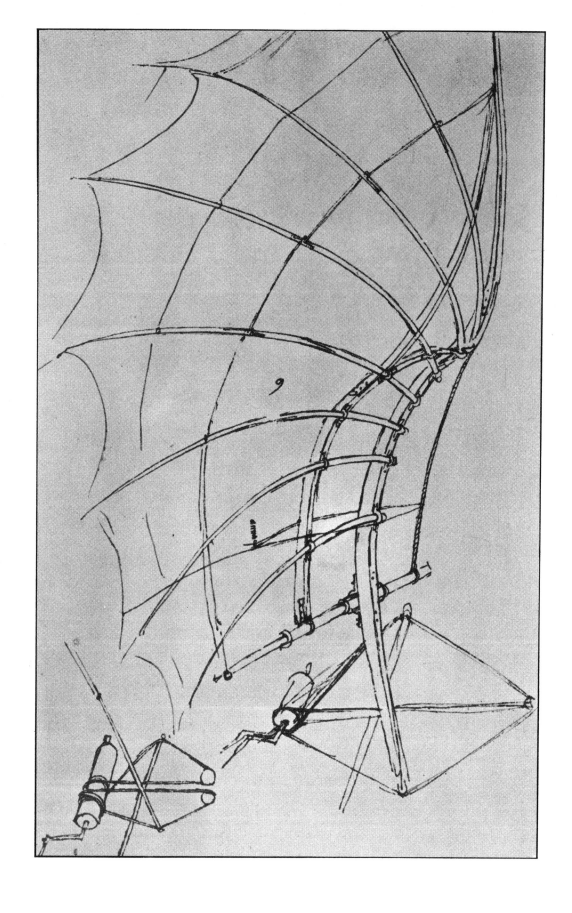

Leonardo da Vinci. *Crank device for manipulating wings*–Codex Atlanticus. Note: Leonardo did not have a letter reversal problem. It was his means of coding his notes and illustrations.

6

GA1506

The Great Falcon and The Yellow-Gold Rabbit

Fairy Tale: Stories are generally simple with profound meanings. Fairy tales concern the adventures of characters in a supernatural or mysterious world.

Here is the beginning of a fairy-tale type of story. Finish the story with an unexpected ending.

The Great Falcon and the Yellow-Gold Rabbit

by _____

There lived, once upon a time, a great falcon who traveled among the canyons and valleys to find the yellow-gold rabbit. For he believed, as did all his brethren, that eternal life would be given to the bird whose talons made the kill. The great falcon became so intent upon this mission that he thought of little else.

Now the yellow-gold rabbit was a very clever rabbit, for he never made a permanent home nor did he allow the wind to carry his scent. He was such a speedy and expeditious rabbit that he could easily escape predators. Sometimes, for the joy of it, he would simply run in circles around coyotes until they became so dizzy they could not recover their senses for many hours. And by that time, the yellow-gold rabbit was nowhere to be found.

On one particular day, the great falcon was enjoying magnificent wind currents above Red Canyon. He enjoyed gliding, for his wings were truly great wings. Sometimes he was mistaken for an eagle when he glided at great altitudes. On that particular day the yellow-gold rabbit was enjoying lunch which was a patch of watercress in a shallow stream.

The great falcon was awakened from his reverie when he suddenly saw yellow-gold movement in the Red Canyon. He wasn't sure what it was at first. He lowered his great wings for a closer look at the yellow-gold thing in the shallow stream.

For information on the exercises refer to the Appendix.

The Great Falcon and the Yellow-Gold Rabbit
by _____

_____

_____

_____

_____

_____

_____

_____

_____

_____

_____

_____

_____

_____

_____

_____

_____

_____

_____

_____

_____

_____

_____

_____

_____

_____

Reproduce this page for additional story pages, if needed. For information on the exercises refer to the Appendix.

Science Fiction Satire

Satire: The use of humor to express foibles or shortcomings in things.
Science Fiction: Fantasy based on varying degrees of scientific facts.

Write a satire on science fiction. But first, determine the basic outline of your story by selecting choices from these various components:

Science Fiction Satire

by _____

Determine a hero!

(Select one.)
____ a happy android with artificial intelligence
____ a brilliant scientist
____ a friendly alien visitor from outer space
____ a space cadet from earth
____ a young computer whiz
____ yourself

Determine a companion for your hero!

(Select one.)
____ an aspiring actress
____ a retired magician
____ an unemployed wizard
____ a pet boa constrictor
____ a dog named Toto
____ a small Hobbit

Determine a villian who will attack your hero!

(Select one.)
____ a giant deadly spider
____ an icky thing with a big brain
____ a fleet of enemy spaceships commanded by D. Vader
____ an evil-tempered Saturnalian
____ an invisible swamp creature
____ a sleepy and hungry mastodon awakening from a deep freeze

For information on the exercises refer to the Appendix.

Science Fiction Satire

by _____

Determine where the attack will take place!

    (Select one.)

        ____ The Golden Gate Bridge in San Francisco

        ____ The Grand Canyon

        ____ NASA's Mission Control in Houston

        ____ Wrigley Field in Chicago

        ____ The San Diego Zoo

        ____ The United Nations Building in New York City

Determine a reason why your hero and companion are where they are!

    (Select one.)

        ____ delivering a coded message there

        ____ taking a vacation there

        ____ visiting friends there

        ____ ran out of fuel there

        ____ on a business trip there

        ____ took the wrong flight

Determine a reason why the villain wants to attack you!

    (Select one.)

        ____ because you represent everything good

        ____ long-time rival

        ____ would make headline news

        ____ to eat you

        ____ boredom and nothing else to do

        ____ because of a contractual arrangement with the evil empire

Determine the outcome of the attack or the resolution of the conflict!

    (Select one.)

        ____ Use an environmentally safe material to immobilize the villain.

        ____ Decide to postpone the conflict and reschedule at reasonable ticket prices.

        ____ A duel to the end with your choice of weapons.

        ____ Negotiate a settlement.

        ____ Get some back-up help from Starfleet for catapulting the villain into space.

        ____ You fall in love with the villain.

        ____ Use a laser to kill it.

        ____ The villain destroys you in some hideous manner.

        ____ Tranquilize the villain with a chemical; then alter its mind from evil to good.

        ____ Use magic to defeat it.

        ____ Strangle it with a snake.

        ____ Your choice (describe).

For information on the exercises refer to the Appendix.

GA1506

Science Fiction Satire

by _____

_____

_____

_____

_____

_____

_____

_____

_____

_____

_____

_____

_____

_____

_____

_____

_____

_____

_____

_____

_____

_____

_____

_____

_____

_____

_____

Reproduce this page for additional story pages, if needed. For information on the exercises refer to the Appendix.

GA1506

Leonardo da Vinci. *Head of horse and study of horses*–Windsor, Royal Collection

Mythology defines us. It tells us who we are and why we are and,
to a certain extent, why we think the way we do.

That's why it is important to study myths.
It is important to learn about us.

12

The First Rainbow

Myths: Stories that usually have their origins in folklore. Traditional myths often made comprehensible what seemed incomprehensible to people.

Create a myth-like story about how rainbows came into being. The beginning of this myth-like story is provided.

The First Rainbow

by _____

There was once a great hunter artist who lived atop the highest mountain in the world. One day he dipped his spear into an urn of many-colored pigments. For some reason he could not stir the solution into the color he wanted. For every time he stirred, the colors would only return to their own hues and not form the dark purple he sought.

Angrily, he _____

_____

_____

_____

_____

_____

_____

_____

_____

_____

_____

_____

_____

_____

_____

_____

And that's how the first rainbow began.

For information on the exercises refer to the Appendix.

Leonardo da Vinci. *Device for knocking over assault ladders*–Codex Atlanticus

14

The Door

Gothic Tales and Stories: They contain elements of mystery and unexpected happenings. Their settings are sometimes in medieval castles encompassed by an atmosphere of fear.

Select a few of these phrases to include within your sentences when finishing the following story.

spider web strands	a broken crossbow
a mysterious chest	an old scroll
an arm bone	a broken gauntlet
a huge boulder	pieces of armor

The Door

by _____

About the middle of July, during the eleventh through sixteenth years of my life, my parents would allow me to visit my grandfather on his estate in Italy. His estate was nestled in the mountains not far from the Austrian border. He lived in a fairly modern French-style chateau, but it wasn't his chateau that interested me. What interested me on his estate was the remaining structure of a medieval castle. Within the castle's great room, at the northeast corner, was a stone stairway that led to what would appear to have been a cellar. At the bottom of the stairway was a sturdy and robust oak door.

It took me several summers to find it. There had been a barricade of useless items in front of the door. Old building stones, timbers, and varied items of debris were there for centuries serving as a obstacle to its discovery.

I was sixteen years old when I was finally able to wedge open the door just enough to peer through that darkened threshold. From the light of my flashlight, I saw

_____

_____

_____

_____

_____

_____

_____

_____

_____

_____

_____

For information on the exercises refer to the Appendix.

The Door

by _____

Select a few of these phrases to include within your sentences.

a flighty feeling of dizziness,
a rancid smell of decay,
the musty air of centuries past
a repulsive network of spidery webs,

Excitedly, I grabbed a timber from the floor and began to wedge the door for a wider opening–an opening I could go through. After squeezing through the door opening, I was overwhelmed by . . .

_____

_____

_____

_____

_____

_____

Needing fresh air, I_____

_____

_____

And then I, _____

_____

_____

The rest of this story is rather frightening, for I have never experienced anything like it nor would I ever want to again. I am fortunate to be here to tell it.

_____

_____

_____

_____

_____

For information on the exercises refer to the Appendix.

Exercise 5
continued

The Door

by _____

_____

_____

_____

_____

_____

_____

_____

_____

_____

_____

_____

_____

_____

_____

_____

_____

_____

_____

_____

_____

_____

_____

_____

_____

_____

Reproduce this page for additional story pages, if needed. For information on the exercises refer to the Appendix.

Leonardo da Vinci. *Studies of expressions for Battle of Anghiari*–Budapest, Museum of Fine Arts

18

The Elevator Scene

Script: The interaction between actors or actresses in a play. A playwright tells a story through the speech of the characters in the play.

Scenario: A working script that includes the dialogue spoken by the actors, the setting and the various technical arrangements dictated by the scene.

Provide a script of conflict between the first and second characters in this scenario.

The Elevator Scene

by _____

The scenario is an elevator in a high-rise building. Two occupants share a ride to the 90th floor.

First: *Enters the elevator first. Looks disapprovingly at the appearance of second entering the elevator carrying a battery-operated stereo. First punches the 90th floor button, retires to the far corner, and mumbles . . .*

Filthy elevator, isn't it?

Second: *Also punches the 90th floor button and retires to the other far corner, turns on a station, and says . . .*

_____

_____

_____

_____

First: _____

_____

_____

_____

For information on the exercises refer to the Appendix.

GA1506

The Elevator Scene

by _____

Second: _____

_____

_____

First: _____

_____

_____

Second: _____

_____

_____

First: _____

_____

_____

Second: _____

_____

_____

First: _____

_____

_____

Second: _____

_____

_____

Reproduce this page for additional story pages, if needed. For information on the exercises refer to the Appendix.

The Yarn

Yarns and Tall Tales: Stories told in common language about impossible happenings.

Select a theme from one of the following and stretch it into an outrageous and unbeliev-able yarn:

How an elephant's trunk became the first fire truck.
How a dinosaur's sneeze started breezes.
How a grandfather's clock became the first wristwatch.
How an anteater invented the first trumpet.
How a ticklebone was discovered.
How a spider became a spider monkey.
How a hole became the Grand Canyon.

The beginning sentences of the yarn are provided. Finish it in the style provided!

The Yarn

by _____

(Write your theme selection on the first blank below.)

She says to me, she says, "Do you know how _____

_____?"

And I says, "Nope!" "Well," she says, "It started like this. _____

_____

_____

_____

_____

_____

_____

_____

_____

_____

_____

_____

_____

_____

_____

For information on the exercises refer to the Appendix.

GA1506

The Yarn

by _____

_____

_____

_____

_____

_____

_____

_____

_____

_____

_____

_____

_____

_____

_____

_____

_____

_____

_____

_____

_____

_____

_____

_____

And she says to me, "That's how it all happened!" And I says, "Thanks a lot, I think."

For information on the exercises refer to the Appendix.

Hundreds of Ways to See the World Through Haiku

Script: A brief poem of seventeen syllables. Formal Japanese haiku does not rhyme. It has three lines of five, seven, and five syllables.

In constructing columns of haiku lines, we can form hundreds upon hundreds of sensory-oriented poems. In this exercise alone there will be 719 choices. Add the correct syllabic count of haiku lines to the blanks in order to create 719 choices.

Example: (1-3-2)

Wild cherry blossom,
What made you fall silently
In the dark meadow?

Example: (10-3-8)

Shy little songbird,
What made you fall silently
At this hour in time?

Example: (6-1-10)

Silent Butterfly,
Where is your bright color now
In the twilight hours?

Hundreds of Ways to See the World Through Haiku
by _____

First lines (5 syllables only)

1. Wild cherry blossom
2. Bright chrysanthemum
3. Crimson maple leaf
4. Melodic starlight
5. _____
6. Silent butterfly
7. _____
8. Small lonely cricket
9. _____
10. Shy little songbird

Second lines (7 syllables only)

1. Where is your bright color now
2. Where will you be tomorrow
3. What made you fall silently
4. Next to this old traveled path
5. Awakens bright memories
6. _____
7. A softly shining poem
8. _____
9. Serenade us with your song
10. _____

Third lines (5 syllables only)

1. In the morning air
2. In the dark meadow
3. In the valley stream
4. _____
5. On this autumn day
6. On this dreary day
7. _____
8. At this hour in time
9. _____
10. In the twilight hours

My Favorite haiku is:

For information on the exercises refer to the Appendix.

I'm often asked by teachers, "How does one become a writer?" Almost anyone can become a writer. Not everyone can write. In attempting to teach children to write, I define perimeters not unlike the perimeters on the exercise sheets in this book. For example, in the exercise across from this page, curiosity and motivation are established early and so is the conflict. I give them half a story and the ownership to it. I think this is important because ownership is important to writing.

I'm like a mother bird teaching a fledging to fly. There are safeguards and stages and perimeters to it all. Before I ask for a complete short story, I'll give students partially done stories that contain certain perimeters. And within those perimeters, I give options to them. And at some point in time, when they're ready, they fly.

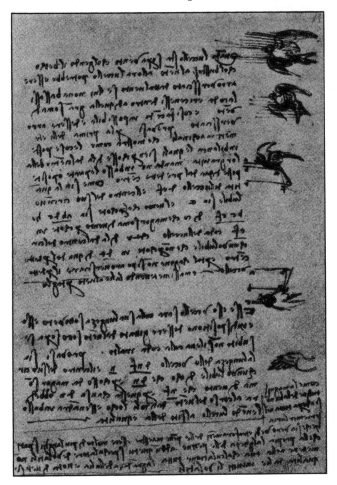

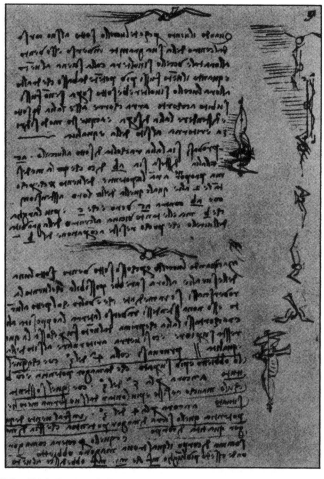

Leonardo da Vinci. *Codex on the flight of birds*–Institut de France.

A Short Story

Short Story: A fictional story which develops a single episode from beginning to end in a limited space.

Make this incomplete short story complete by making additions. Try to take the episode, with your additions, to a smooth conclusion. Read the incomplete story first; then think about what might be added.

A Short Story

by _____

He never shared the experiences nor could he. Who would believe him? The other night he saw it again in the western sky above the mesa. It rose quickly and _____

_____

_____

_____

And then it was gone. He stayed for a brief moment to see if it would come back. It didn't. He got home as quickly as he could, as quickly as his limp would allow him.

At school, the next day, he couldn't concentrate. His mind was still in the night sky. The pulsating lights of what he saw subdued everything into nothingness. "Jack!" He felt a sudden jolt. He heard laughter throughout the room. He saw an angry Mrs. Angelo.

"Jack, _____

_____

_____

_____."

Awkwardly, he _____

_____

_____

_____

For information on the exercises refer to the Appendix.

GA1506

A Short Story

by _____

After detention, he avoided phoning home. He would walk the three miles. He needed time to think–time to contemplate and speculate without interruption. What was it? Was it some kind of a Hopi festival on the mesa? Was it some experimental or secret government project? Was it hallucinations on his part? Was it extraterrestrial? Was it something else?

"Jack, I had a phone call from Mrs. Angelo. She said your mind has been somewhere else other than English class the past few days."

"Huh?"

He went to his room, tossed his books on a chair, and laid on his bed.

She worried about him more since the accident. He had to give up a lot of things he enjoyed because of the leg. And she desperately wanted him to do well in school. He had such a good mind–a mind of curiosity and depth. She was going to mention the detention, but decided to wait until a later time–maybe in the morning. She knew that three miles on a permanent disability had to be debilitating to him.

"Jack, you'd better hit the books tonight after dinner." Her voice awakened him.

During dinner, Jack_____

_____

_____

_____

_____

_____

Afterwards, he_____

_____

_____

_____

_____

_____

_____

For information on the exercises refer to the Appendix.

GA1506

A Short Story

by _____

Jack had difficulty sleeping. He stared restlessly at the window trying to dislodge the compulsive replay of his thoughts. He could not rest his mind to find sleep.

Jack arose from the bed, gathered some clothes, and _____

_____

_____

_____

The air was chilling to his hands and face as he approached the mesa. Then, _____

_____

_____

_____

_____

_____

_____

_____

_____

_____

_____

_____

_____

_____

_____

_____

_____

_____

_____

For information on the exercises refer to the Appendix.

GA1506

A Short Story

by _____

_____

_____

_____

_____

_____

_____

_____

_____

_____

_____

_____

_____

_____

_____

_____

_____

_____

_____

_____

_____

_____

_____

_____

_____

_____

Reproduce this page for additional story pages, if needed. For information on the exercises refer to the Appendix. The concluding paragraph of "A Short Story" is on the next page.

GA1506

A Short Story

by _____

_____

_____

_____

_____

_____

_____

_____

_____

_____

_____

_____

_____

_____

_____

_____

_____

_____

_____

_____

_____

_____

_____

He ran from the mesa. Reeling from the confusion of it all, he tripped on a piece of mesquite wood. He tried to gather some rationality of thought as he got to his feet. But all he could do was renew his frenzied run home.

Run? How could he run? He wasn't able to run, but he was running.

For information on the exercises refer to the Appendix.

Leonardo da Vinci. *Handwritten list of works*—Codex Atlanticus

I like to provide attribute word lists to students. The type of list provided depends on what they are writing. If they are describing characters, they will receive a list of personality attributes accommodating a broad range of personality types. If they are describing objects or things, they will receive a list of physical attribute words. Words such as *porous, spongy, dimensional, flexible,* etc., might be on a list of this type. I want them to have available choices for becoming more articulate and descriptive in their selection of words.

A Novel Beginning

by _____

Novel:	It tells an extended story. Due to the length of a novel, an author can develop characterization, situations, and events to the extent of involving the reader in the developing story.
Character Study:	Describing a character or person's qualities, mannerisms, and behavior for an interesting written portrait.

Imagine the three italicized sentences below are the beginning of a novel. Start the development of a major character known as Suzanne with descriptive words and information. Utilize a few of the words and phrases listed in the left margin to assist you. Be imaginative and descriptive in describing her qualities, actions, mannerisms, and behavior.

A Novel Beginning

by _____

aggressive
aloof
artistic
assertive
beautiful
brash
caring
charming
clever
comical
confident
courteous
creative
forgetful
forthright
fragile-looking
friendly smile
frightened
gentle
graceful
grinning
impish
intelligent
lonely
loud
neatly dressed
nervous
opinionated
petite
piercing eyes
quiet
shy
slender
sophisticated
stunning
suspicious
tall

"Suzanne," you say? Yes, I can recall my first and most vivid impression of her. It was Michael's house some twenty or more years ago.

_____

_____

_____

_____

_____

_____

_____

_____

_____

_____

_____

_____

_____

_____

_____

_____

_____

_____

For information on the exercises refer to the Appendix.

GA1506

It is important, I think, that we as teachers
provide opportunities for students
to integrate their varied portraits of self
into what we ask of them to do.

I think Leonardo was like that.
His varied portraits of self, in addition to his art,
encompassed anatomy, biology, engineering
and invention and so many things.

I think he would have taught in this fashion, as well.
If he taught language, it would have included
mathematics and language.
If he taught mathematics, it would have
included language and history.
Our varied portraits of self should go well
beyond what we are salaried to do.

Leonardo da Vinci. *Feminine headdresses*—Windsor, Royal Collection

An Autobiographical Account
by _____

Autobiography: The story of one's life. The writer looks back on his or her life, selects
certain incidents, and constructs a story around them.

Complete this questionnaire form, determine what incidents and topics are most important on the form, and then write a limited autobiography about them. It is *not* important
to complete each and every statement. Be as *brief* as possible. All that is needed here are
concise words or reminder notes.

An Autobiographical Account
by _____

My proudest day was _____

My greatest surprise was _____

My greatest achievement was _____

My greatest disappointment was _____

My most eventful challenge was_____

My greatest interests are_____

My special skills and talents are _____

My special creations have been _____

My awards have been _____

My accomplishments have been _____

My most memorable time was _____

My most dangerous moment was_____

My most fun experiences are _____

My most treasured moment was_____

My most frightful experience was _____

My greatest commitments are _____

My saddest recollections are _____

My most treasured memories are _____

My greatest ambitions are _____

Select only a few statements; then write a descriptive autobiographical account about
them.

For information on the exercises refer to the Appendix.

GA1506

An Autobiographical Account
by _____

_____

_____

_____

_____

_____

_____

_____

_____

_____

_____

_____

_____

_____

_____

_____

_____

_____

_____

_____

_____

_____

_____

_____

_____

_____

_____

_____

_____

Reproduce this page for additional story pages, if needed. For information on the exercises refer to the Appendix.

Escape

Adventure: These stories have action and excitement. Their plots tantalize you to keep reading.

Portions of this story are provided. Provide what is missing to make it an absorbing, action-filled and exciting adventure story.

Escape

by _____

It was in early February, I believe. Yes, it was just before the great blizzard that we decided to do a preposterous celebration of Groundhog Day. There were four of us, _____, _____, _____, and myself. It was _____ idea to build a huge snow sculpture of a groundhog and celebrate its shadow when the sun appeared.

The groundhog must have been _____ feet tall. Snow clouds were forming and so we gave up on its shadow and the celebration of it. We gathered our packs and cross-country skis and headed for the ranger shelter down the mountain. The sky was looking foreboding and very large flakes were beginning to fall.

Conditions were becoming extremely treacherous. _____ broke a ski on a snow-covered boulder. That slowed us down considerably. We still had two hours before nightfall to get to that shelter.

When we got there, the first few things we did were to _____

_____

_____

_____

_____

_____

_____

_____

_____

_____

_____

For information on the exercises refer to the Appendix.

Escape

by _____

A major disappointment was the discovery that our battery-powered radio transmitter wasn't working. Apparently when _____ fell, due to the broken ski, something else became broken too! Unfortunately for us, the transmitter was in _____ backpack.

The wind howled like a wolf pack and conditions were worsening. It was on the third night that we heard an incredible roar. It was so powerful that everything within the shelter and the shelter itself jostled and trembled.

_____ yelled, "Avalanche!"

Make a choice from the following.
Check (√) one.

_____ • The shelter becomes buried in snow and huge boulders. They become imprisoned by the landslide.

_____ • They run from the shelter in search of protection from the landslide.

_____ • The shelter is destroyed and there's one survivor, the narrator of the story.

_____ • Your choice: _____

Now complete the adventure story with some solution or resolution to this conflict with nature.

_____

_____

_____

_____

_____

_____

_____

_____

_____

_____

_____

_____

For information on the exercises refer to the Appendix.

GA1506

Escape

by _____

_____
_____
_____
_____
_____
_____
_____
_____
_____
_____
_____
_____
_____
_____
_____
_____
_____
_____
_____
_____
_____
_____
_____
_____
_____

Reproduce this page for additional story pages, if needed. For information on the exercises refer to the Appendix.

GA1506

Leonardo da Vinci. *The Warrior Drawing*—Milan, Ambrosiana

Caricatures, often accompanied by jokes or descriptive explanations, have been a mode of expression for centuries. Rembrandt did it. Da Vinci did it and so did early tribes and clans in the form of pictographs.

Language can be expressed in many varied ways. To teach any language effectively requires explorations into various modes of expression, for language is expression. Sometimes, as teachers, we forget that.

Whole language, whole mind is language.

GA1506

Cartooning

Cartoons: Using graphic art and words, cartoons may entertain or satirize a broad range of topics from politics to everyday encounters.

Satire: The use of humor to express foibles or shortcomings in things.

Caption: Words accompanying a cartoon, illustration, photograph, or subtitle in a motion picture.

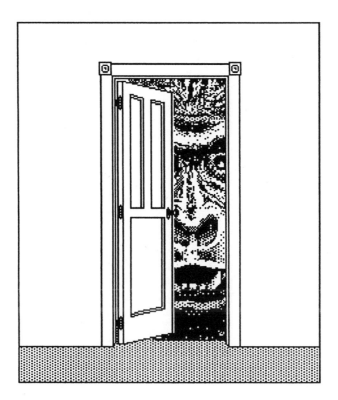

BOYS AND GIRLS, WE HAVE A VERY SPECIAL GUEST TODAY
WHO WILL SPEAK ON THE TOPIC OF ANIMAL RIGHTS.

On paper list all of the precise or specific topics you can think of about school. These things may include procedures you must follow in assembly, cafeteria, fire drills, classrooms and special classes like music, art, physical education, etc. Then think far out for the purpose of satirizing one of these topics with a drawing and a related caption. Do it!

For information on the exercises refer to the Appendix.

The graphic illustration was created within the MacPaint Program of Claris ©, Version 2.0, 1987, Claris Corporation.

GA1506

We
are but oaks
from
whose branches
acorns fall.

Some become trees
that tower above landscapes.

Some become feed
for those who
live on landscapes.

We are here
for nurturing those who tower
and those who don't.

Leonardo da Vinci. *Rebus idaeus*—Windsor, Royal Collection.

Ads

Advertisements: Utilizing words and/or visuals, advertisements are intended to sell goods or services.

Persuasive Writing: Writing that is intended to convert people to a particular conviction, belief, or point of view. Persuasive writing can be found in advertisements, endorsements, editorials, essays, and various other genre.

Use persuasive writing in doing an ad on one of these:

a cola
athletic shoes
a shampoo
toothpaste
pizza
aspirin
a restaurant
a clothing store
a travel agency
a cosmetic
an automobile dealership
a motion picture
a television show
a dietary product

For information on the exercises refer to the Appendix.

The graphic illustration was from the MacPaint Program of Claris ©, Version 2.0, 1987, Claris Corporation.

41

GA1506

Leonardo da Vinci. *Drawing of a dog*—Windsor, Royal Collection.

Hound Dawg and Po Possum
by _____

Children's Literature: This is a broad field of stories, poems, folk tales, and picture books of various kinds. Children's literature must be simple, yet still convey the elements of good writing.

Dialect: A regional variety of language distinguished by pronunciation, grammar, or vocabulary.

Hound Dawg and Po Possum
by _____

Hound Dawg said to Po Possum one day, "Po, where ye all git that strange tail of yours? Hit sure a long 'un!"

Po, always deliberate and thoughtful, said, "Well now, Hound Dawg, hit looks like ye all be a needin' to knows how hit all got started."

Hound Dawg knew he was in for a long story. So he just circled the ground a couple of times and lay down in a comfortable fashion.

Finish the story using as many dialect words as you can from the glossary.

Glossary
ain't = no
disputin' = disagree
eat'in = eat
git = get
hit = it
hollered = yelled
lookin' = looking
knows = know
'lowed = knew
a needin' = needing
nuttin' = nothing
reckon = believe
squawkin' = noise
takin' = taking a
'un = one
ye = you

_____
_____
_____
_____
_____
_____
_____
_____
_____
_____
_____
_____
_____
_____

For information on the exercises refer to the Appendix.

The author wishes to acknowledge the teachers, staff and service personnel of the Summerfield Elementary School, Summerfield, North Carolina, for indoctrinating his mind with their unique patterns of a regional dialect. He reckons he hadn't bin the same since hit happen'.

Hound Dawg and Po Possum

by _____

Glossary

ain't = no
disputin' = disagree
eat'in = eat
git = get
hit = it
hollered = yelled
lookin' = looking
knows = know
'lowed = knew
a needin' = needing
nuttin' = nothing
reckon = believe
squawkin' = noise
takin' = taking a
'un = one
ye = you

_____
_____
_____
_____
_____
_____
_____
_____
_____
_____

_____
_____
_____
_____
_____
_____
_____
_____
_____
_____
_____
_____
_____

Reproduce this page for additional story pages, if needed. For information on the exercises refer to the Appendix.

GA1506

The Biographical Organizer

Biography: A story of someone's life written by someone who either knew the person or researched information and facts on that person. The purpose of a biography is to present the events in a person's life in an informative and interesting way.

Character Study: Describing a character or person's qualities, actions, mannerisms, and behavior for an interesting written portrait.

Use this format to assist you in preparing notes for a biographical presentation. Refer to your notes while you make your presentation.

Subject's Name: _____

Resources Used

_____

_____

_____

_____

_____

_____

Character Study Remarks (Personality Traits or Behavior) on the Subject

_____

_____

_____

_____

_____

_____

_____

_____

_____

_____

_____

For information on the exercises refer to the Appendix.

The Biographical Organizer
by _____

The Subject's Major Achievements

_____
_____
_____
_____
_____
_____

Major Influences on the Subject's Life

_____
_____
_____
_____
_____

A Major Obstacle, Disappointment, or Conflict in the Subject's Life

_____
_____
_____
_____
_____
_____

Your Thoughts and Feelings Toward the Subject

_____
_____
_____
_____
_____
_____

For information on the exercises refer to the Appendix.

GA1506

Artist
Philosopher
Mathematician
Astronomer
Physicist
Linguist
Essayist
Writer
Researcher
Caricaturist
Designer
Musician
Craftsman
Architect
Physiologist
Landscaper
Engineer
Inventor
Biologist
Botanist
Mechanic
Geologist
Geographer

Leonardo was all of the
 above and then some.
Holistic?
Whole-minded?
Perhaps the greatest ever!

Portrait of Leonardo by unknown painter—Florence, Uffizi Gallery

47

GA1506

Improvements on anything are made by adding or subtracting or combining or reducing or reversing or adapting or modifying it in some fashion. Everything! And that includes teaching.

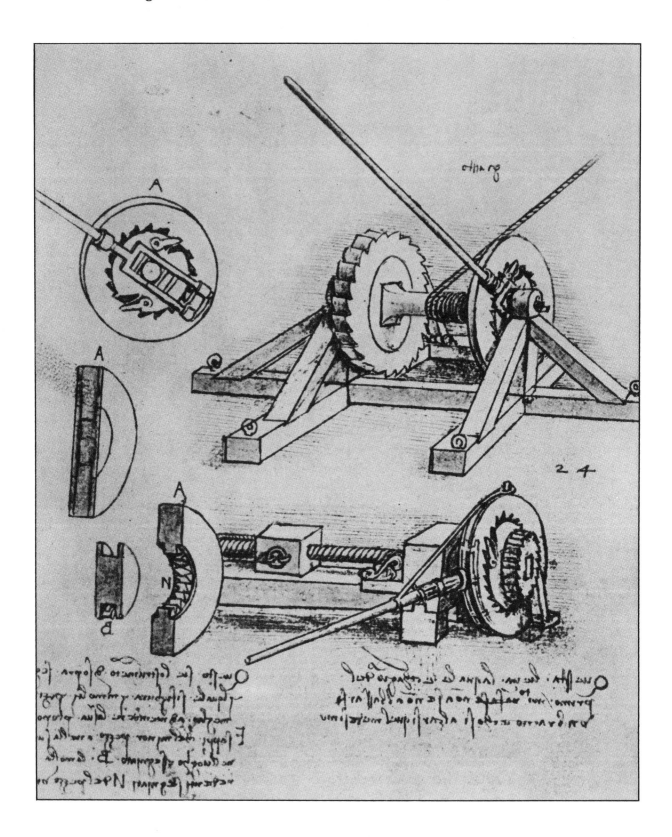

Leonardo da Vinci. *Winch with ratched control*—Codex Atlanticus.

Turn on Dynamatron Rex!

Technical Writing: A broad range of specialized writings that includes manuals, guides, procedures, reports, proposals, directions, explanations or instructions on mechanical, industrial or vocational topics, items or things.

Jargon: The specialized or technical language of a trade. Sometimes referred to as meaningless or nonsensical talk.

Write a nonsensical or meaningless description about how to operate a fictitious machine called the Dynamatron Rex. Use several of the listed jargon words in your description and add some of your own. Underline the jargon words used.

A brief example:

After assembling Dynamatron Rex, make sure the <u>ejector mechanism</u> is in the off position before pushing the <u>starter button</u>. Failing to do so may launch Dynamatron Rex into an orbital path around Venus. Set the <u>dial</u> to a medium setting so the <u>ball bearings</u> are exposed to a lesser degree of <u>friction</u> . . . .

- starter button
- heating element
- ejector mechanism
- cartridge
- filter
- friction
- dial
- ball bearings
- fuses
- monitor
- carburetor
- conveyor belt
- blinker
- spring action
- meters
- thermostat
- odometer
- gears
- photoelectric cell
- programmer
- sensor
- transformer
- antenna loop
- pneumatic system
- synthesizer
- volume
- tuner
- dialog box
- toll-free number

Turn on Dynamatron Rex!

by _____

_____

_____

_____

_____

_____

_____

_____

_____

_____

_____

_____

_____

_____

_____

_____

_____

For information on the exercises refer to the Appendix.

GA1506

Turn on Dynamatron Rex!

by _____

Keeping your technical written description of Dynamatron Rex in mind, illustrate a comical drawing of it. Label some of the parts with jargon words.

Dynamatron Rex

- starter button
- heating element
- ejector mechanism
- cartridge
- filter
- friction
- dial
- ball bearings
- fuses
- monitor
- carburetor
- conveyor belt
- blinker
- spring action
- meters
- thermostat
- odometer
- gears
- photoelectric cell
- programmer
- sensor
- transformer
- antenna loop
- pneumatic system
- synthesizer
- volume
- tuner
- dialog box
- toll-free number

For information on the exercises refer to the Appendix.

GA1506

Vampire Parody[ise]

Parody: Writing that mimics or ridicules a type of story or writing style.

Write a two-page parody by ridiculing a Dracula type of character in an absurd and outrageous way. Consider using some of the phrases at the bottom of the page within the context of your writing.

Vampire Parody[ise]

by _____

The Count, looking into the mirror, gives a distorted and grotesque smile as he watches his fangs grow. Grabbing the fluoride, plaque-fighting tube of _____

_____

_____

Wesley, the Count's manservant, raps nervously on the bathroom door and stutters, "Ma Ma Ma Ma Master, _____

_____."

The Count _____

_____

_____

_____

_____

_____

_____

_____

_____

_____

_____

_____

_____

• hypnotic stare • howling dogs • world of the undead
• ravenous hunger for a vein •menacing-looking

For information on the exercises refer to the Appendix.

Vampire Parody[ise]

by _____

Reminder: This is a parody. Ridicule it! Make it funny!

_____

_____

_____

_____

_____

_____

_____

_____

_____

_____

_____

_____

_____

_____

_____

_____

_____

_____

_____

_____

_____

_____

More phrases to consider using:

• stealth and cunning • foreboding full moon • soul-stalking • piercing scream • a muffled groan • an unearthly sight • sinister stare • morbid fascination • ghastly grin • appalling odor • beady-eyed • loathsome glimpse • eerie feeling

For information on the exercises refer to the Appendix.

Interviewing Mr. B.

Fantasy: Stories set in an unreal world. Fantasy is based purely upon the richness of an author's imagination.

Interview: A record of a conversation between an interviewer and a subject. The interviewer's intent is to provide for readers an overview and understanding of the subject being interviewed.

Transcript: A record of a conversation. Transcripts may be derived from interviews, trials, or someone's recollections.

Imagine that a huge brontosaurus was discovered in a remote area of the world. Also imagine that during a three-year debriefing period by government agents and scientists, you were chosen to interview "Mr. B." During the brontosaurus' debriefing period, several overzealous scientists taught Mr. B. to speak in several different languages including your own. Provide a written transcript of a mock interview between you and Mr. B. Since you are the first interviewer, think of some highly important questions to ask Mr. B.

Interviewing Mr. B.

by _____

Interviewer: I'm not surprised by your size, but I thought all dinosaurs were green or gray or something in-between.

Mr. B.:   Not at all. We came in many different colors. We sort of blended in with our surroundings. That's why I have brown and green spots all over me. I lived among plants and rocks.

Interviewer: _____

_____

_____

Mr. B.:   _____

_____

_____

Interviewer: _____

_____

_____

For information on the exercises refer to the Appendix.

GA1506

Interviewing Mr. B.

by _____

Mr. B.: _____
_____
_____

Interviewer: _____
_____
_____

Mr. B.: _____
_____
_____

Interviewer: _____
_____
_____

Mr. B.: _____
_____
_____

Interviewer: Well, thank you, Mr. B. It certainly has been enlightening for me and I'm sure for our readers, as well! You've corrected many misconceptions we had of you.

For information on the exercises refer to the Appendix.

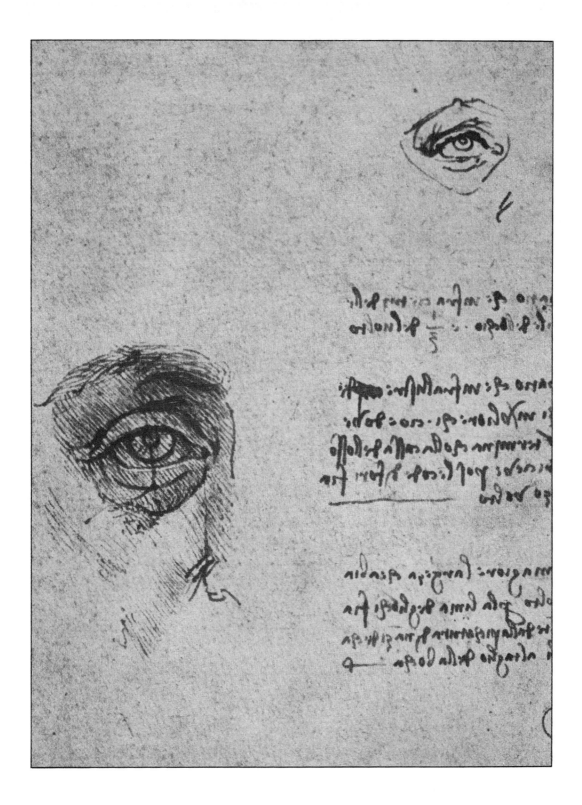

Leonardo da Vinci. *Studies of the eye*—Turin, Royal Library

Sometimes I take students through a vast array of activities that call for observation. In every case, I tell them to caress the object with their eyes and minds. At times, I have them write descriptions of it. At times, I have them illustrate their conceptions of it. In either case, I say softly, ". . . Caress it with your eye and mind."

Within my work, I make an effort to accommodate visual thinkers. There are many of us. We like space on printed pages so our conceived mental images may dance with words. It is rarely that I will fill a page completely with words. Visual thinkers will draw images next to words or in place of words to give depth to the meanings of things.

Was Leonardo a visual thinker? Just take a look!

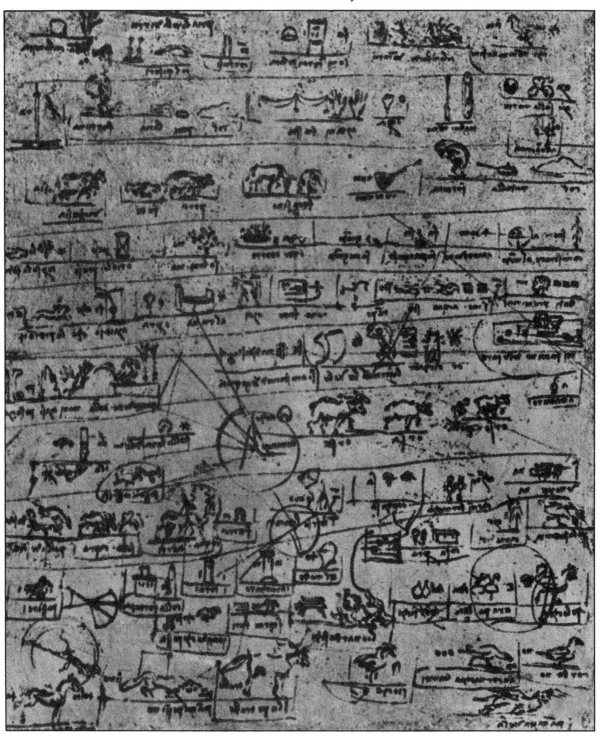

Leonardo da Vinci. *Rebuses and figured words*—Windsor, Royal Collection

A Western

Westerns: Stories set in the Old West usually consisting of one or more of the following: cowboys, Indians, cattle rustlers, bad men, lawmen, prospectors, cavalry, cowgirls, saloon keepers, etc.

Format

Select a hero or heroine from this list.
(Check √ one.)
____ Miss Mary, the school marm
____ Sundancer, a noble chief
____ Wild Bill, an ex-desperado turned good
____ Lt. Johnston, a young cavalry officer
____ Miss Annie, a retired sharpshooter from a wild West show
____ Gunther Gun, the town marshall
____ Sunrise, the beautiful daughter of Sundancer
____ Clint, a stranger in town

Select a villain from this list.
(Check √ one.)
____ Slick Sam, a gambler
____ Miss Gloria, a greedy saloon keeper
____ Bad-eye Bart, a gunslinger
____ Billy Joe, a notorious cattle thief
____ Mrs. Rattler, a widow who buried six husbands
____ Jim Hiccup, an ex-marshal turned bad
____ Damien, a demented poker dealer
____ Sly, a stranger in town

Select a setting where a conflict will take place.
(Check √ one.)
____ the town bank
____ the saloon
____ the corral
____ the schoolhouse
____ a ranch
____ the jail
____ the only street in town
____ on the range
____ an abandoned gold mine
____ the fort
____ the corral
____ the Indian encampment north of town

Select a conflict for the setting.
(Check √ one.)
____ Villain wants revenge from a past deed.
____ Villain is caught cheating at cards.
____ Villain is jealous over a woman.
____ Villain is jealous over a man.
____ Villain has robbed a bank.
____ The town's not big enough for the two main characters.
____ Villain is wanted by the authorities.
____ Villain is caught stealing a cow.
____ Villain hates good and honorable people.
____ Villain wants to set the range afire.
____ Villain is wanted for stealing a horse.
____ Villain wants to be the fastest gun in the West.

Now write a Western story from the format choices you selected. Give the story a happy ending. You may add minor characters to your story.

For information on the exercises refer to the Appendix.

GA1506

A Western

by _____

_____

_____

_____

_____

_____

_____

_____

_____

_____

_____

_____

_____

_____

_____

_____

_____

_____

_____

_____

_____

_____

_____

_____

_____

Reproduce this page for additional story pages, if needed. For information on the exercises refer to the Appendix.

Leonardo's Aerial Machine

Historical Fiction: A fictional story or account interwoven amid fictional and actual persons, associations, and events in history.

Leonardo's Aerial Machine

by _____

He sat in Leonardo's studio awaiting his bidding. The master had spent years on the drawings, notes, and the model constructions that emerged from his thoughts. No one in the world, he thought, had the intellect of his master. His current effort may place him in history as the greatest inventor ever. Lorenzo felt blessed to be his young apprentice.

On the studio floor, amid earthen pots of colored pigments and brushes sat huge stacks of paper coded in a reverse style of writing on the flight of birds. And on tables were dissections and reconstructions of wings. Lorenzo tried desperately to keep his master's studio somewhat in order, but it was an endless and hopeless effort.

Lorenzo was terrified of the secret he knew. If it were not for the master's self-portrait and mirror he used to create it, the codex would have remained a secret belonging only to its creator. One late afternoon, while Lorenzo was cleaning the studio, he saw the transformation of the codex into a legible language. It was through the mirror's reflection that he saw it. In a mirror's reflection written letters are reversed. If letters are written in a reverse fashion, the mirror will revert those letters back to their normal condition. There were many in Milan who would pay a handsome price to have possession of the master's codex decoded. He would not betray Leonardo. But what if Leonardo knew what Lorenzo knew? He would be discharged immediately, Lorenzo was sure.

One startling illustration and its decoded message remained in Lorenzo's mind, for he could not erase the image nor the message. Often in the small room that was his place of boarding, the image would dance in his head. Leonardo referred to the illustration as "The Aerial Twist" in code. And it appeared to Lorenzo that the blades rotating on a vertical cylinder could twirl in a rapid fashion. Did the master create a machine that would transport a person by air to remote areas of the land? In this year of 1488 there had been great discoveries and inventions, but nothing known would compare to this.

Lorenzo, one evening by candlelight, drew the image that had captivated his mind for so long. Carefully, he replicated his master's drawing and the codex that accompanied it. He had a wonderful visual memory–one that retained incontestable detail. Upon completion, he studied it. How ingenious, he thought.

Suddenly, the bedroom door opened. And there stood Leonardo da Vinci. Lorenzo was paralyzed with fear. The master approached the desk and saw Lorenzo's replica and the translation of the codex.

For information on the exercises refer to the Appendix.

GA1506

Leonardo's Aerial Machine
by _____

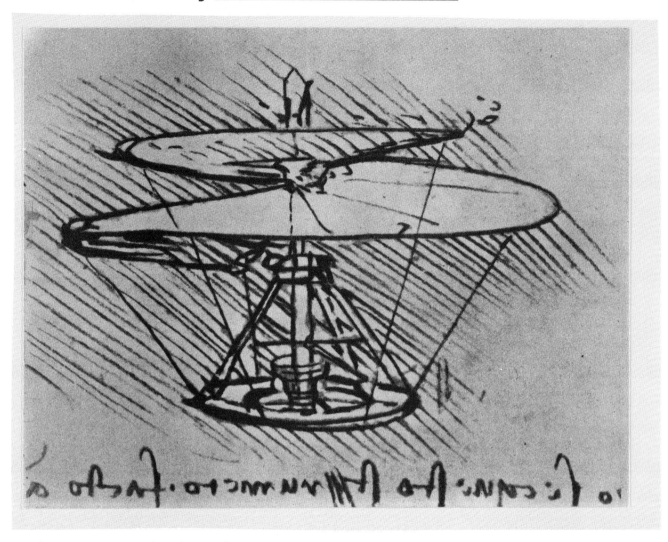

Select a way to resolve the conflict, then complete the story.

- Lorenzo is discharged in disgrace.
- Lorenzo is discharged and attempts to sell Da Vinci's idea to other inventors in Milan.
- Lorenzo convinces Da Vinci that he meant no harm, that he was just intrigued by the master's ingenuity.
- Da Vinci forgives Lorenzo and allows him to assist him in building his "Aerial Twist" machine.
- Da Vinci realizes that he must bring someone into his trust. Upon his death, who would benefit from his work if no one had access to the translation of the codex? Perhaps Lorenzo would be the one.
- _____ (Your choice)

For information on the exercises refer to the Appendix.

Leonardo's Aerial Machine

by _____

_____

_____

_____

_____

_____

_____

_____

_____

_____

_____

_____

_____

_____

_____

_____

_____

_____

_____

_____

_____

_____

_____

_____

_____

_____

_____

Reproduce this page for additional story pages, if needed.

For information on the exercises refer to the Appendix.

GA1506

A Brief Vignette on Passion

Passion, for me, was always the treasure. The first viable look was never in cumulative records; it was to find the passion. And it mattered not if it was origami or baseball cards or rocketry or something far removed from what I was salaried to teach. For if I found passion, I found access to a mind. If the access was through origami, I would start the child with technical writings about constructing origami. The passageway from technical writing to other genres of writing or anything was made easier.

Passion is such an important thing, for it foretells of high creative potential. One attribute of creativeness is passion. And within passion is commitment–a commitment to do something just for the joy and the intrinsic desire of doing it. For within the desire to do it is the passion for the processes involved. When we master anything, we must first master the processes that will enable us to do it. Find the passion, and you'll find access to the universe.

Teresa Amabile speaks eloquently on passion and vision within the young creative child in her book, *Growing Up Creative* (Amabile, 1989). This book is an extremely important book for parents and teachers of young children.

GA1506

A Vignette

Vignette: A short, usually descriptive literary work.

Finish this vignette (pronounced vin-yet) by providing an ending.

A Vignette

by _____

Have you ever wondered how certain words originated? How about the word *maroon*? Maroon is a very dark red. Maybe someone held an apple to moonlight and said, "It's not really bright red anymore. I think I'll just add two more letters to the letters in *moon* and call this new color maroon." Perhaps someone was on a deserted island with nothing to eat except a decaying apple (which also, by the way, turns from red to maroon) and said, "I feel like the apple. I must be marooned."

How about the word _____? _____

_____

_____

_____

_____

_____

_____

_____

_____

_____

_____

_____

_____

_____

There are many words to choose from in order to complete your vignette. Here are a few interesting ones to consider:

chopsticks	clubhouse	dictatorship	foolhardy
handshake	hummingbird	mischief	napkin
nightmare	overlook	passage	prattle
prong	scatter	stretcher	waistline

For information on the exercises refer to the Appendix.

GA1506

Leonardo da Vinci. *Head of a woman*—Parma Gallery

Concrete Poetry

Concrete Poetry: The shape in which words are aligned adds to the meaning of the message.

Cut alphabet letters or words from a newspaper to make a collage of a concrete poem. Afterwards, experiment with reading your poem from different angles or perspectives.

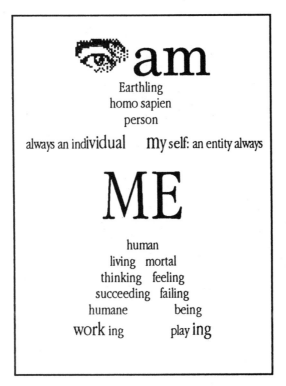

Possible Topics:

something for sale
a skyscraper
a motion picture
a sport
an automobile
a news item
yourself
a newsmaker
a headline
political cartoon

For information on the exercises refer to the Appendix.

GA1506

A Concrete Poem

by _____

Use the grid to help align your letters and words.

For information on the exercises refer to the Appendix.

News Reporting

Reportage: Reporting of first-hand newsworthy events by a news reporter.

Write a make-believe news report about an orangutan that escaped from a truck and entered a shopping mall. Good reporting deals with these questions: who? what? why? where? when?

Orangutan Goes on Destructive
Shopping Spree in Local Mall

(AP) An escaped orangutan sent hundreds of screaming shoppers into a frightened frenzy yesterday afternoon at _____

_____

_____

_____

_____

_____

_____

_____

_____

_____

_____

_____

_____

_____

_____

_____

_____

_____

_____

Reported by _____

For information on the exercises refer to the Appendix.

Sometime back, when I was living in Texas, I would go on a routine basis to the Armand Bayou Nature Center. I did this for a couple of reasons. Sometimes I'd walk silently through a woodland path and sometimes it was to see the baby alligator. Just the attendants, who confided in me, and I knew about the gator. It was in a small pond outside the compound. There are those who destroy life, so I never shared the secret. I imagine, if it's still alive, it's somewhere else in a very mature state of being.

On one afternoon, at the bayou, I met a tall, gray-haired man by the name of Campbell Loughmiller and his wife, Lynn. We started talking and it wasn't long into the conversation that I learned that he and his wife were writers. They gave me one of their books. It was entitled *Big Thicket Legacy*. It's a beautiful book of primary sources that they compiled from the folks who lived in the Big Thicket.

It has always seemed to me that every minuscule experience of my being, at some given point in time, reappears. This time it is the setting of the Big Thicket for a story legend on the next page.

Leonardo da Vinci. *Studies for monument to Francesco Sforza*—Windsor, Royal Collection

68

GA1506

Brown Leggett and the Yellow Pine Bat

Legends: Usually fictional stories that are based upon some truth occurring in the past. Legends are handed down from generation to generation. Storytellers usually exaggerate these stories to make them more interesting.

Brown Leggett and the Yellow Pine Bat

by _____

It was maybe ten years or so after Abner Doubleday invented the game that it got to Big Thicket Country in East Texas. And it wasn't too long after that a clearing was made from among the yellow pines just east of Cypress Creek. The soil was sort of sandy there and it made for a pretty fair ball diamond.

The folks in Big Thicket raised their corn, sweet potatoes, and cane and hunted deer and bear in addition to some lumbering. These folks were an independent lot who built their cabins on high ground, who farmed and worked just enough to get by without much assistance from anyone.

There was this feud between two families that had gone on for a long time. At one time they were shooting at each other, but someone had decided that maybe a weekly baseball game between the two families would be a bit safer. And so on Saturday afternoons, the Walker and the Leggett families played baseball on the sandlot. Folks from the Thicket would travel miles to see those games.

Now the Walker and Leggett families had many cousins and other kin and there never was a shortage of players. There was one Leggett, Brown Leggett was his name, who had some kind of a reputation as a logger. He was a huge man who spent most of his time in the woods. They said he could split a yellow pine log with no more than three swings. No one had ever seen him play baseball, but many would give a jug of sorghum just to see him swing a bat.

It was about mid-October in 1898, when it was decided that the final baseball game for that season would be played. Twenty-four games had been played between the two families, and each family had twelve wins and twelve losses.

On the Saturday of the last game, Brown Leggett came out of the woods. And on his shoulder was this huge, shiny, yellow, pinewood club. They say it was about four and a half feet long and it must have weighed five pounds.

Note: Remember that legends are exaggerated stories. Finish the story by creating a written legend of Brown Leggett and his yellow pine bat.

For information on the exercises refer to the Appendix.

Brown Leggett and the Yellow Pine Bat
by _____

_____
_____
_____
_____
_____
_____
_____
_____
_____
_____
_____
_____
_____
_____
_____
_____
_____
_____
_____
_____
_____
_____
_____
_____
_____
_____
_____
_____

Reproduce this page for additional story pages, if needed. For information on the exercises refer to the Appendix.

GA1506

Stream of Consciousness

Stream of Consciousness: Thoughts and images that flow, uninterrupted, from a writer's mind.

Take a few minutes to record on note paper everything that enters your mind. Then put them together as a written piece. My example is on the left. Write your stream of consciousness on the right side. Use another sheet of paper if necessary.

My Stream of Consciousness

by _____

It's raining! There's water streaming down the sidewalk and road pavement. Stream of consciousness? How do I do this? Wish I was fishing a trout stream, but not today; it's raining. I'm fishing for ways to do this. Just give an example of my own stream of consciousness and encourage kids to do the same. I've never asked for a stream of consciousness in a classroom. There are no places to paragraph these things; they just ramble. I'm tired and I've been at this computer since 5:30 this morning. The ideas are still coming. What happens when they stop? Is it like death? I don't want to give up this book. I don't want to finish it. I want to write it forever. But this place is a mess; there's more paper on the floor than on the shelves. Books everywhere and I've been stepping on them for the past week. I want the sun and I want this book. I don't have any suns in this book. Where do I go from here? Do I do an exercise on writing a synopsis or a memoir or what? I don't know. My lamp reminds me of a sun. I hear trains. This town is full of trains–always the trains. They used to wake me. I sleep through them now. Wet trains on wet tracks, streams of rain, a stream of consciousness, trout streams, ocean streams, jet streams . . .

For information on the exercises refer to the Appendix.

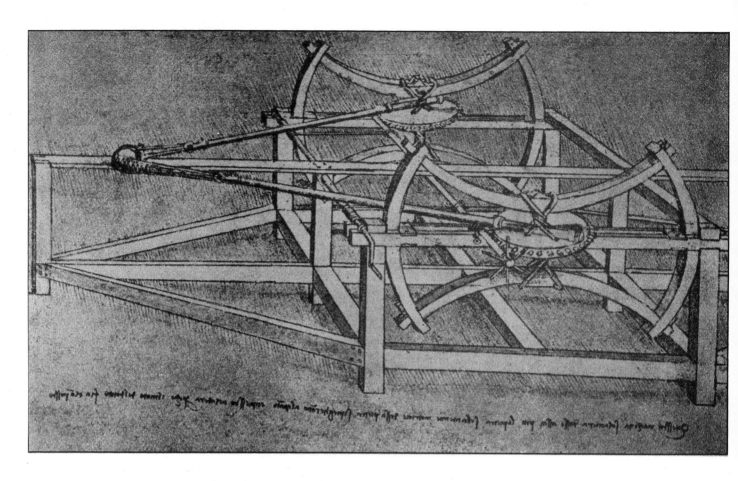

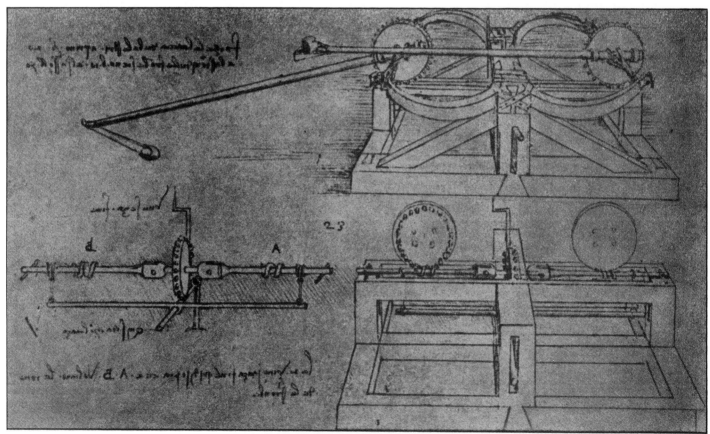

Leonardo da Vinci. (Above) *Machine for throwing rocks and bombs.* (Below) *Catapults and crossbows*—Codex Atlanticus.

72

Synopsis

Synopsis: A summary of the theme of a more extended piece of writing.

The following is an extract from the autobiography of Plenty-Coups (1848-1932), Chief of the Crow Nation. The extract can also be found in the book, *Touch the Earth*, by T.C. McLuhan. Read it carefully; then write a synopsis of it.

Chief Plenty-Coups

"... I could see our country was changing fast, and that these changes were causing us to live very differently. Anybody could now see that soon there would be no buffalo on the plains and everybody was wondering how we could live after they were gone. There were few war parties, and almost no raids ... White men with their spotted-buf-falo[1] were on the plains about us. Their houses were near the water-holes and their villages on the rivers. We made up our minds to be friendly with them, in spite of all the changes they were bringing. But we found this difficult, because the white men too often promised to do one thing and then when they acted at all, did another.

They spoke very loudly when they said their laws were made for everybody; but we soon learned that although they expected us to keep them, they thought nothing of breaking them themselves. They told us not to drink whiskey, yet they made it them-selves and traded it to us for furs and robes until both were nearly gone. Their Wise Ones said we might have their religion, but when we tried to understand it we found that there were too many kinds of religion among white men for us to understand, and that scarcely any two white men agreed which was the right one to learn. This bothered us a good deal until we saw that the white man did not take his religion any more seri-ously than he did his laws, and that he kept both of them just behind him, like Helpers, to use when they might do him good in his dealings with strangers. These were not our ways. We kept the laws we made and lived our religion. We have never been able to understand the white man, who fools nobody but himself."

[1]spotted-buffalo means cattle

For information on the exercises refer to the Appendix.

Synopsis

by _____

Before writing the synopsis, think . . .

Who wrote it?
What was it about?
Why was it written?
To whom was it addressed?

Keep in mind that a synopsis is a summary.

Chief Plenty-Coups

_____
_____
_____
_____
_____
_____
_____
_____
_____
_____
_____
_____
_____
_____
_____
_____
_____
_____

Phrases that could be used in writing a
synopsis of Chief Plenty-Coups' extract:

encroachment of Crow lands
hypocrisy of
eloquently and somberly
devastated a way of living

For information on the exercises refer to the Appendix.

GA1506

Memoirs

Memoirs: Written recollections by authors of events in their lives.

Here is an example of what could be found in a memoir. Read it and then think of a single event in your life that would lend itself to a memoir.

A Memoir

I can recall my first frightening and heroic impressions of them. I was only five, but the huge gray mammoths sent me scurrying inside. I bounded the steps of the front porch like the man of steel–faster than a speeding bullet.

Opening the front door just wide enough for my right eye to see the awesome sight, I saw four of them. Huge beasts, they were, swaying their long trunks rhythmically in the early morning light. Men with barbed poles kept them together by the hydrant. A wrench was used by one man to loosen a cap, and water came forth in walloping gushes.

I watched breathlessly as my mind transported the man of steel to the heart of Africa. The barking of neighborhood dogs suddenly became the cries of monkeys scurrying for the uppermost branches. And Emma Lou's cat, flashing across the street in panic, was a lioness giving her territory to the gray invaders.

And then it was over. The hydrant cap was secured and the gray mammoths lumbered down Fifth Street–towards the tents and the distant music of the calliope. The man of steel, disillusioned by the sudden exit, opened the door wider. And with the return to the street of Emma Lou's cat and the barking stilled, the man of steel bravely and without hesitation ventured from the house to inspect his front sidewalk. The sidewalk, crushed in hundreds of fragmented pieces of concrete, bore the proof. The man of steel is a friend to all good and kind creatures large and small–even those who created havoc for roller skates in the years that followed.

For information on the exercises refer to the Appendix.

GA1506

A Memoir

by _____

_____

_____

_____

_____

_____

_____

_____

_____

_____

_____

_____

_____

_____

_____

_____

_____

_____

_____

_____

_____

_____

_____

_____

_____

_____

_____

_____

_____

Reproduce this page for additional story pages, if needed. For information on the exercises refer to the Appendix.

GA1506

A Comic Essay

Essay: A short piece of writing on a topic.

Write an essay on comic books.

A Comic Essay

by _____

Comic books come in various categories ranging from superheroes to small lovable animals to almost ordinary kinds of characters. Some of my favorite comic book characters have been _____

_____

_____

_____

_____

_____

_____

My earliest comic books consisted of _____

_____

_____

_____

_____

_____

_____

I think today's comic books _____

_____

_____

_____

_____

_____

_____

For information on the exercises refer to the Appendix.

A Comic Essay

by _____

_____

_____

_____

_____

_____

_____

_____

_____

_____

_____

_____

_____

_____

_____

_____

_____

_____

_____

_____

_____

_____

_____

_____

_____

_____

Reproduce this page for additional story pages, if needed. For information on the exercises refer to the Appendix.

78   GA1506

Great improvements are always stimulated by imagination and need. It is with imagination and need that we should reinvent education, for education is in need of invention.

Children must be given opportunities to apply, modify, play, and invent. For within this comes the intrinsic desire to know and the curiosity to find.

If I could change anything in the world, it would be apply, modify, play, and invent for every child. I'd do it for the intrinsic desire to know and the curiosity to find.

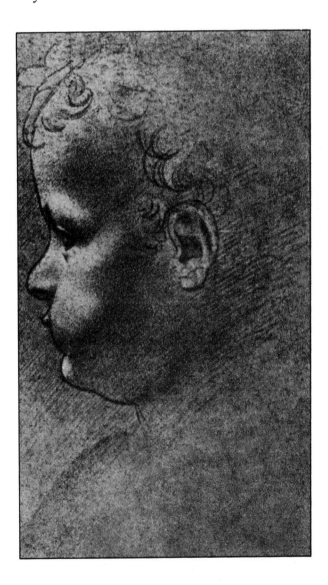

Leonardo da Vinci. *Drawing of an infant's head*—Paris, Louvre

There are two great and extraordinary resources in this country of ours.

One is the child whose unlimited resources are not being tapped.

The other is the elderly whose resources could be tapped.

I've learned more from them than from any book or from any institute of learning.

Leonardo da Vinci. *Old man's profile*—Turin, former Royal Collection

GA1506

A Chronicle Tale

Chronicles: Fictional or nonfictional stories consisting of incidents told in the order they happened.

Fantasy: Stories set in an unreal world. Fantasy is based purely upon the richness of an author's imagination.

Make the incompletions complete for a chronicle!

A Chronicle Tale

by _____

Some miles north of the crater and towards the peninsula lived the old recluse. No one knew his name and very few had ever seen him. As Adam approached his hut, he saw him. The recluse (Describe him!) _____

_____

_____

_____

_____

_____

_____

Startled at Adam's sudden and unexpected intrusion, he raised his walking stick in an aggressive fashion. Adam sat down near a tree and said to him in a calm and congenial tone, " _____

_____

_____

_____

_____

_____

_____

_____ ."

He didn't mention the unicorn. He just wanted to gain his confidence. From the corner of his eye, Adam could see the rough-hewed remains of what appeared to be, at one time, a stable. The old recluse just stared wordless and emotionless at him.

For information on the exercises refer to the Appendix.

GA1506

A Chronicle Tale

by _____

Awkwardly, Adam began talking about himself. He told the recluse that _____

_____

_____

_____

_____

_____

_____

_____

_____

_____

After what seemed a millennium of time, the old recluse motioned Adam to follow him. Inside the hut, Adam sat on a stump next to an untidy table of tools, a plate, and a mug. The old recluse took an iron kettle of water and hung it on a hook in the fireplace. With cedar shakes, he started a fire. All this time, he kept an eye on Adam. But Adam saw a glimmer of a smile emerge from his wrinkled lips.

From an earthen pot on the floor, the recluse gathered a pinch of shredded leaves and placed them in the mug. He watched intently as Adam sipped the hot herbal tea. The hut was (Describe the inside of the hut!) _____

_____

_____

_____

_____

_____

_____

_____

_____

_____

For information on the exercises refer to the Appendix.

GA1506

A Chronicle Tale

by _____

Adam saw a twinkle in the old man's eye. Leaning on his walking stick, he slowly and haltingly rose to his feet. It was at that moment Adam realized the man could not speak. The recluse pointed his stick towards the door.

Adam wasn't sure if the old recluse was dismissing him or what. But the old man grabbed his elbow for additional support and led him outside onto a path. (Describe their walk along a wooded path to a reflecting point.) _____

_____

_____

_____

_____

_____

_____

_____

_____

_____

_____

_____

_____

_____

_____

There on the far side of the pond stood the unicorn. Magnificent, Adam thought. Absolutely magnificent! This was even better than he planned–a speechless old man and the unicorn. Oh, so easy!

Recall that a chronicle consists of incidents occurring in the order they happen. Finish the chronicle in one of these ways.
- Adam takes the unicorn.
- Adam leaves without the unicorn.
- Adam decides to assist the recluse in protecting the unicorn.
- (Provide a different choice.) _____

_____

For information on the exercises refer to the Appendix.

GA1506

A Chronicle Tale

by _____

_____

_____

_____

_____

_____

_____

_____

_____

_____

_____

_____

_____

_____

_____

_____

_____

_____

_____

_____

_____

_____

_____

_____

_____

_____

_____

_____

Reproduce this page for additional story pages, if needed. For information on the exercises refer to the Appendix.

GA1506

The Appendix

Key Instructional Words for Promoting a Whole
Mind Approach to Literature and the Language Arts

Examples:

Questioning: What *analogy* might be appropriate for this scene?
In what ways might the qualities of the story's heroine be *debatable*?

Objectives: Students will *build* sets for the first act of Hamlet.
Students will write *captions* for provided political cartoons.

Account (for)
Adapt
Add
Adjust
Alter
Amend
Analogy (make an . . .)
Analyze
Anecdote (add an . . .)
Anticipate
Arrange
Articulate
Assimilate
Broaden
Build
Calculate
Captions (write . . .)
Caricature (draw a . . .)
Cartoon (make a . . .)
Cast (develop a . . .)
Cause (cause/effect)
Character (develop a . . .)
Characteristic
Characterization
Characterize
Cite
Clarify
Classify
Collaborate
Collect
Combine
Commentary (make a . . .)
Compare
Compile
Complete
Compose
Conceive
Conclude
Concoct
Concur
Condense
Conflict (determine the . . .)
Connect
Consequences (determine the . . .)

Consider
Construct
Contrast
Create
Debate
Deduce/Determine/Differentiate
Define
Dramatize
Draw
Edit
Effect (cause/effect)
Elaborate
Eliminate
Elocution
Elucidate
Embellish
Emphasize
Emulate
Engage
Enlarge
Enumerate
Enunciate
Essay (write/read an . . .)
Estimate
Etch
Events (determine . . .)
Evidence (provide . . .)
Exaggerate
Examine
Example (give an . . .)
Excerpt
Exclude
Expand
Experiment
Explain
Explore
Expose
Express
Extend
Extract
Fabricate
Facts
Fantasize
Farce (develop a . . .)

Feelings (toward something)
Fictionalize
Finish
Fix
Flaws (in dialogue or script?)
Fluent
Focus
Foretell
Formulate
Full-length
Gather (data)
Generalize
Generate
Give
Graphics (insert . . .)
Guess
Harmonious (story elements?)
Headline
Humanize (objects, things, etc.)
Hypothesis
Hypothetical
Ideas
Idealistic
Identify
Illicit
Illogical (what's . . . ?)
Illustrate
Illustrations (do or add . . .)
Image
Imagery
Imaginary
Imaginative
Imagine
Implication
Implicit
Impromptu
Improve
Improvisation
Improvise
Inconsistencies (find . . .)
Induce
Infer/Inference
Initiate
Innuendo

Inquire
Insert
Inspect
Install
Instigate
Instruct
Interchange
Interpret
Interrogate
Interview
Introduce
Intuit
Invent
Investigate
Involve
Journalistic (styles)
Judge
Justify
Juxtaposition
Know
Layout (do a . . .)
Learn
Lengthen
Liken/Likeness
Link
Linear
List
Listen
Locate
Logically
Longitudinal
Lyrical (make it . . .)
Make
Make-believe
Mark
Master
Match
Measure
Memorize
Merge
Mention
Mime
Mimic
Miniaturize

Model (make a . . .)
Moderate
Modify
Monologue (do a . . .)
Multiply (choices)
Name
Narrate
Negotiate (ideas)
Nominate
Note
Notice
Objections (find . . .)
Obscure (what is . . . ?)
Observe
Obtain
Offer
Opinions
Opposite
Oratorical
Oratory
Organize
Original
Originality
Paint (sets, mural, scenes)
Panel (form a . . .)
Pantomime
Paradox (find the . . .)
Paraphrase
Participate
Perform
Perpetrate
Personify (make it personal)
Persuade
Peruse
Philosophize
Pick
Picture (it)
Place
Plan
Play (a role)
Plot
Poetic (make it)
Point out
Ponder
Portfolio (develop a . . .)
Portraits (character . . .)
Portray
Practice

Predict (outcomes)
Premise
Prepare
Prescribe (what's needed)
Present
Preside (over a discussion)
Presume
Pretend
Preview
Prioritize
Probability (chances?)
Probe
Problem (determine the . . .)
Proceed
Procure
Produce
Product (create a . . .)
Project
Pronounce
Proof (find . . .)
Propose
Prove
Publish
Punctuate
Puns (write . . .)
Qualify
Quips (create . . .)
Quote
Rank (in importance)
Rate
Rationalize
React
Read
Reason
Reassemble
Rebuff
Rebuild
Rebuke
Recite
Recognize
Recollect
Recommend
Reconcile
Reconsider
Reconstruct
Record
Recount
Re-create

Refer
Reflect
Refute
Rehearse
Reiterate (information)
Reject
Relate
Remark
Remember
Remove (something)
Rename (title, characters)
Repeat
Reproduce
Reread
Rescind
Research
Resolve
Resources (find . . .)
Review
Revise
Satirize
Scenario (write a . . .)
Script (write a . . .)
Search/Seek
Select
Separate
Sequel (create a . . .)
Sequence (place in . . .)
Shorten
Show
Similarities
Simplify
Simulate
Sketch
Skim
Solve
Speak
Spontaneously (react . . .)
State
Story
Strategy (develop a . . .)
Study
Submit
Summarize
Superimpose (something else)
Support
Suppose
Supposition

Surmise
Symbolize
Symposium
Syntax (analyze . . .)
Synthesis
Tabulate
Testimonial (write or give a . . .)
Testimony
Theme (determine a . . .)
Theory (develop a . . .)
Think
Transact
Transfer
Transform
Translate (meaning, words)
Transmit
Transpose
Try
Underline
Understand
Use
Utilize
Verbalize
Visualize (it)
Web (it)
Write

Note:
This two-page list of words may be used as an idea-stimulating device for developing lesson plan ideas and strategies.

Information and Objectives on the Lesson Exercises

Retain or modify or add or broaden or revise the stated objectives according to the capabilities of students and instructional expectations. The objectives are not intended to be appropriate for all academic and achievement levels.

"Of Course . . ."
Exercise 1

Objectives:
- Students will be able to articulate one or more elements of a mystery story.
- Students will be able to define what a motive is.
- Students will use written words to elaborate and embellish on an incomplete story to make it complete.
- Students will present their completed stories as monologues to selected other students.
- Students will utilize comprehension skills of supposition, inference, and analysis in completing the stories.

"Of Course . . ." is a comical spoof on mystery stories, but it still retains the basic elements of that genre, such as suspense, a detective, a crime, and a motive for that crime. Make sure that students read the provided information before they begin to write. Consider placing students in groups for the purpose of presenting their story as a monologue, that is, a speech by one actor or presenter.

The Great Falcon and the Yellow-Gold Rabbit
Exercise 2

Objectives:
- Students will be able to write an appropriate and sequential ending to a fairy-tale type of story.
- Students will be able to cite one or more characteristics associated with fairy tales.

This fairy-tale type of story is intended to encourage students to provide some simple message or meaning. Encourage students to use descriptive language much in the style of the paragraphs provided. Although it is unlikely that many unexpected endings will be realized, acknowledge those students who do provide an extraordinary ending.

Science Fiction Satire
Exercise 3

Objectives:
- Students will be able to plan, from choices given, an outline of a potential satirical science fiction story.
- Students will write a satirical science fiction story containing characters, setting, conflict, and resolution of conflict.
- Students will be able to define the terms *satire* and *science fiction*.

Science Fiction Satire will score high in motivation for writing purposes. Give students an opportunity to share their stories with others.

GA1506

The First Rainbow
Exercise 4

Objectives:
- Given the first paragraph of a myth-like story, students will be able to provide a written synthesis of a total story.
- Students will be able to hypothesize about the origins of myths.

Encourage students to recall examples of myths previously read. Follow those responses with a discussion centered around the definition of a myth cited on the exercise page.

The Door
Exercise 5

Objectives:
- Students will be able to express the major elements of Gothic tales and stories.
- Students will be able to select phrases from provided choices to create a harmonious association with story elements.
- Students will use written words to elaborate and embellish on an incomplete story to make it complete.
- Students will be able to extend the elements of mystery and suspense, provided at the story's beginning to the story's conclusion.

Encourage students to read what is provided on the exercise sheets first; then explore possibilities for the development of conflict which they'll have to resolve. Emphasize or dramatize the last provided paragraph in the exercise: *The rest of this story is rather frightening, for I have never experienced anything like it nor would I ever want to again. I am fortunate to be here to tell it.* Ask, "What perimeters or boundaries are explicit here?" (The narrator must survive.)

The Elevator Scene
Exercise 6

Objectives:
- Students will be able to write an interactive script between two fictitious characters.
- Students will be able to relate what a scenario is.
- Students will be able to provide a written conflict within the scenario.
- Students will be able, if asked, to act and/or direct an original scenario.

Act out selected scripts. Allow the writer of a chosen script to direct the scenario, establish props and circumstances relating to the setting. Afterwards, critique the various scenarios as a class. Also discuss how the various conflicts might be resolved; for example, in what ways might a peaceful settlement be established between the two characters?

General discussion topics:
What are the differences between a page of script and a book page of fiction?
What would be more difficult, transforming a book into a script or transforming a script into a book? Explain.
What problems might a playwright have that a book author wouldn't have?
In what ways might you integrate "The Elevator Scene" into a play of a larger context?

GA1506

The Yarn
Exercise 7

Objectives:
- Provided with seven choices, students will select a theme for writing a yarn or tall tale.
- Students will be able to express one or more elements associated with yarns or tall tales.
- Provided with a given style of expression, students will write the yarn or tall tale in that style.

Instructions:
Select the yarns that meet all three of the below-mentioned criteria. Then decide on the best of the best. Write the best of the best on a piece of paper and give it to your teacher.

Suggested Criteria:
- expressed in "common language"
- tells about an impossible or outrageous happening
- good sentence structure, grammar, and spelling

Hundreds of Ways to See the World Through Haiku
Exercise 8

Objectives:
- Students will add choices on a morphological synthesis matrix in order to multiply selection choices.
- Students will use a morphological synthesis matrix to formulate haiku poems.
- Students will record their favorite haiku from hundreds of potential choices.

Spend some time on this exercise, for it provides a strategy (morphological synthesis) by which multiple ideas can be generated (Stanish, 1986, 1988, 1990). It is important to tell students about this strategy, for it can be used in developing choices on story characters, settings, and story conflicts too!

Encourage students to share their favorite haiku with the total class.

A Short Story
Exercise 9

Objectives:
- Students will be able to state the limitations of a short story.
- Students will use written words to elaborate and embellish on an incomplete story to make it complete.
- Students will be able to provide a resolution to the story's conflict.

This exercise is a highly motivating one requiring imagination and suspense. Provide adequate time, either at home or school, for its completion. Then, in either small or large groupings, encourage students to share their short stories with others.

GA1506

A Novel Beginning
Exercise 10

Objectives:
- Students will be able to surmise the advantages of a novel over other genre.
- Students will be able to develop a character study of a character named Suzanne through attribute selection.
- Students will be able to write a characterization of Suzanne.

Discuss the advantages of a novel over a short story from the perspective of a writer. Also discuss the importance of characterization as it relates to a novel, for example, the importance of developing the main characters through word selection and usage. Direct attention to the list of words on the exercise page. Encourage students to use some of these words in describing Suzanne within the context of the beginning pages of a hypothetical novel.

An Autobiographical Account
Exercise 11

Objectives:
- Students will be able to orally discriminate between an autobiography and a biography.
- Given an outline of open-ended questions, students will be able to select topics appropriate for writing a descriptive autobiographical account.

Either through posting the accounts on a wall or a desk, or through an oratorical means, provide a means by which they are shared. Afterwards, ask: Why are there more biographies in a library than autobiographies? (Privacy; one famous individual might warrant dozens of different biographies, while normally, he or she may only write one; not every famous individual is a writer, etc.)

Escape
Exercise 12

Objectives:
- Students will be able to cite elements associated with adventure stories.
- Students will be able to prioritize options in order to select an event leading to the story's completion.
- Students will utilize comprehension skills of supposition, inference, and analysis in completing the story.
- Students will use written words to elaborate and embellish an incomplete story to make it complete.

This story will motivate students to write. Provide adequate time within class or use it as a homework assignment. Duplicate adequate copies of the last exercise page for those students who will extend or expand the conflict and the resolution of that conflict. Some completed stories may warrant acknowledgement through some sort of a school-wide exposure or display.

Before the writing process, encourage students to either illustrate story scenes, select magazine illustrations, or utilize computer clip art for enhancing their stories' appeal.

Encourage students to list adventure stories they've read. Have them analyze their story with adventure stories read. In what ways are they similar in excitement, action, and the motivation to read until completion?

Cartooning
Exercise 13

Objectives:
- Students will be able to define cartoon and satire.
- Students will be able to conceive of a topic to satirize.
- Students will be able to illustrate and provide a caption to a cartoon.

Bring examples of political cartoons to class and discuss how satire is compatible to cartoons. After completing the exercise, post the cartoons on a classroom wall.

Ads
Exercise 14

Objectives:
- Students will be able to reason the purposes of an advertisement.
- Students will be able to select an advertisement topic from choices given.
- Students will be able to use persuasive writing in developing a hypothetical ad.

Bring examples of newspaper ads to class and ask students what the persuasive elements are in these ads. After developing the purposes of persuasive language, encourage students to create a make-believe ad.

Hound Dawg and Po Possum
Exercise 15

Objectives:
- Students will be able to state one or more elements associated with children's literature.
- Students will cite a purpose or purposes for the use of written dialect.
- Students will be able to select and compose dialect for the purposes of story writing.
- Students will be able to write a children's literature type of story.

For those students who are really motivated to use dialect words, here are some more:

a-laughin' = laughing	makin' = making
awfulest = bad	r'ared = raised
be'in = being	runnin' = running
bin = been	standin' = standing
fixin' = going to	tendin' = attending to
fin'ly = finally	throw'd - threw
lettin' = let	workin' = working

Provide opportunities for reading and sharing of the completed stories. They should prove to be both entertaining and interesting. Investigate books in the library that contain dialect.

The Biographical Organizer
Exercise 16

Objectives:
- Students will be able to state the purposes of a biography.
- Students will be able to differentiate between an autobiography and a biography.
- Students will be able to compile notes for a brief character study on a given personality.
- Students will be able to complete a biographical format.
- Students will be able to articulate a presentation using written notes compiled in a provided biographical format.

Provide the Biographical Organizer as an instrument to assist students in preparing classroom presentations on biographical material. Emphasize the need for notes as opposed to complete sentences and lengthy written information. The major purpose of the format is to provide some consistency on biographical topics so that comparisons and contrasts can be formed on personalities studied.

Turn on Dynamatron Rex!
Exercise 17

Objectives:
- Students will be able to state the elements of technical writing.
- Students will be able to differentiate between vocational jargon and meaningless jargon as it applies to writing.
- Students will be able to write a nonsensical account of a fictitious machine utilizing provided jargon.
- Students will be able to graphically illustrate elements of the fictitious machine they described.

This exercise has three purposes:
1. To familiarize students with the broad scope of technical writing.
2. To familiarize students with jargon.
3. To provide students with some playful and entertaining elements of writing.

Do not restrict students to use just the word choices offered. Encourage them to use technical and jargon words of their own choosing as well.

Vampire Parody[ise]
Exercise 18

Objectives:
- Students will be able to explain the rationale for writing parodies.
- Students will be able to write a brief story using a parody style of writing.

Draw attention to the first two sentences provided in the story. The incomplete second sentence calls for a brand of toothpaste for a Dracula-like character. This should set the tone for parody and ridicule the monster-type of story found in books and movies. You may have to remind students to keep their stories ridiculous and amusing.

Provide some means of sharing or exhibiting the parodies written.

Interviewing Mr. B.
Exercise 19

Objectives:
- Students will be able to articulate one or more elements of stories based on fantasy.
- Students will be able to combine an interview format with transcript.
- Students will be able to write a fantasy story using the elements of an interview format.

Before beginning this exercise, discuss the importance of the interview question. The use of the "why?" question should be limited to appropriate times only. Good interview questions are open-ended, that is, they allow the respondent to respond and explain. Encourage students to share their transcripts in small groups and then discuss within those groups what is known and is not known about dinosaurs.

A Western
Exercise 20

Objectives:
- Students will be able to list the common characteristics associated with Western stories.
- Students will be able to select characters, setting, and plot from provided information prior to writing a Western story.
- Students will be able to write a Western story.

This will be a motivating and fun writing assignment for students. Find ways to exhibit their stories. The happy-ending constraint within the exercise is there for providing conflict resolution. Insist they do it; then afterwards explain the reason it was there.

Leonardo's Aerial Machine
Exercise 21

Objectives:
- Students will be able to comprehend and paraphrase a provided page of a story.
- Students will be able to differentiate certain elements of fact from fiction on a provided page of a story.
- Students will be able to define historical fiction.
- Students will be able to provide a written resolution of conflict to a provided plot.

Note: The illustration on the second page of this exercise is a photograph of Leonardo's concept of a flying machine. He called it an "aerial screw." His concept became the earliest known forerunner of today's helicopter.

It is very important for students to fully comprehend the first page of this exercise. It may be advisable to have someone read it while remaining class members follow the script.

After completing the exercise, provide some time to discuss historical fiction. Challenge students to find facts on the first page of the exercise.

Facts the author used in writing the fictional scenario:
- Leonardo did have a studio in Milan prior to and after the year 1488.
- He did have a codex (a coded manuscript) written in a reverse style.
- He did have apprentices.
- He did investigate the probability of building aerial machines in that period of time.

A Vignette
Exercise 22

Objectives:
- Students will be able to express the purpose of a vignette.
- Students will be able to complete a partially completed vignette.
- Students will be able to express elaboration and/or originality of thought in their completed vignettes.
- Students will be able to, if asked, cite various topics appropriate to vignettes.

Encourage students to use humor and insight in completing this assignment. The suggested words at the bottom of the exercise page are only suggestions. There are many words to choose from either through recollection or with a dictionary.

Concrete Poetry
Exercise 23

Objectives:
- Students will be able to define concrete poetry.
- Students will be able to create a concrete poem utilizing varying typefaces or styles of print and images from provided newspapers.
- Students will display their completed products.

Provide old newspapers, scissors, and glue to students. Draw attention to the concrete poem example on the exercise sheet. Read the poem from the top to the bottom. Then read the same poem from the botttom to the top. Indicate that many concrete poems can be read in many different ways.

These poems should be extremely appropriate for display and discussion.

News Reporting
Exercise 24

Objectives:
- Students will be able to write a make-believe news story.
- Students will be able to comprehend reportage as a writing genre.
- Students will be able to articulate the importance of gaining firsthand information on newsworthy events.

Emphasize that effective news reporting addresses the questions of Who? What? Why? Where? and When? Also indicate their news report should be brief and interesting. Have them limit their reports to the space provided on the exercise page.

Some students will ask about the (AP) at the beginning of the paragraph. AP stands for Associated Press. They are to imagine they are reporters for the Associated Press.

Have students read their news items in class.

Ask students, in their opinions, what makes for competent reporting? What makes for inferior reporting?

GA1506

Brown Leggett and the Yellow Pine Bat
Exercise 25

Objectives:
- Students will be able to cite one or more elements associated with stories that are deemed legends.
- Students will be able to provide a written conclusion to a legend type of story.
- Students will be able to use exaggeration within their story for the purpose of interest.

These are several ways to provide an interesting exaggerated conclusion to this legend type of story:
- Brown Leggett swings with such force, the ball tears a hole through his bat.
- Brown Leggett swings and misses the ball. The force of his swing causes tree leaves to fall for twenty square miles.
- Brown Leggett, inadvertently in a mighty swing, lets the bat go and it severs three pine trees.
- Brown Leggett hits the ball with such a tremendous force, the ball becomes a comet. It's known today by astronomers as Leggett comet.

You may want to brainstorm with your class as many exaggerated endings as possible before they begin writing.

Stream of Consciousness
Exercise 26

Objectives:
- Students will be able to explain a writer's stream of consciousness.
- Students will be able to write an abbreviated stream of consciousness.

This may be a difficult exercise for some. Try a three-minute period of time for silence and note taking and a longer period of time for writing.

It is suggested that the stream of consciousness efforts are not shared in a public way. Instead, ask questions like:

Did you find this difficult to do? What made it difficult?
How many different thoughts entered your consciousness?
How many of your thoughts were connected with a previous thought?

Synopsis
Exercise 27

Objectives:
- Students will be able to define *synopsis*.
- Students will be able to write a synopsis from a provided extract.

An example of a synopsis:

Chief Plenty-Coups, a chief of the Crow Nation, writes eloquently and somberly of the changes that took place among his tribe with the encroachment of the Crow lands by settlers and ranchers. He speaks of the differences of thinking, of unkept promises, and the hypocrisy of the white man to the Native American.

Memoirs
Exercise 28

Objectives:
- Students will be able to state a definition for *memoirs*.
- Students will be able to peruse a provided memoir, then recollect and write about an event in their own lives.

To help students recollect an event to write a memoir about, say: Think about an achievement or a disappointment or a special occasion or a special memory or a special surprise or a special challenge or a special vacation or an event that has remained in your memory over time.

A Comic Essay
Exercise 29

Objectives:
- Students will be able to comprehend the purpose of an essay.
- Students will be able to write an essay.

Just in case there are some students who would not care for or would have little interest in the provided topic, provide some of these topics for essay consideration:

- A Computer Game Worth Playing
- A Video Game Worth Buying
- A Hobby Item Worth Collecting
- A Motion Picture Worth Seeing
- An Author Worth Reading
- A Board Game Worth Playing
- A Recipe Worth Making
- A Hobby Worth Pursuing

A Chronicle Tale
Exercise 30

Objectives:
- Students will be able to define a chronicle.
- Students will use written words to elaborate and embellish an incomplete chronicle to make it complete.
- Students will utilize comprehension skills of supposition, inference, and analysis in completing the chronicle.
- Students will be able to select an appropriate conclusion from choices provided to complete the chronicle.

Discuss the differences between chronicles and novels, chronicles and science fiction, and chronicles and other genres. In some respects a chronicle is like a journal or a diary in that events are in a chronological order. Novels, science fiction, and other literary genres may go back and forward in time (flashbacks) within the context of their stories.

Encourage students to read the entire exercise before they begin to write. Provide opportunities for students to share their stories.

GA1506

Sample Test Questions for the Storyscaping Exercises

Moderate Difficulty

1. Stories that contain suspense and crimes would most likely be
   a. adventure stories
   b. mystery stories +
   c. stories containing myths
   d. stories containing legends
   e. biographies

2. Another name for a yarn is
   a. a fairy tale
   b. a legend
   c. a myth
   d. tall tale +
   e. a scenario

3. Simple stories with profound or deep meanings are
   a. fairy tales +
   b. Gothic tales and stories
   c. satires
   d. essays
   e. vignettes

4. Which of the following genres would always be found in a major city newspaper?
   a. essay
   b. parody
   c. reportage +
   d. short story
   e. interview

5. Stories that consist of incidents told in the order they happened are
   a. monologues
   b. biographies
   c. novels
   d. mystery stories
   e. chornicles +

Sample Test Questions for the Storyscaping Exercises

Moderate Difficulty

6. In which of the following genres would you *least* expect to find satire?
   a. a mystery story
   b. an adventure story
   c. a science fiction story
   d. a historical fiction story +
   e. a Gothic story

7. Stories that contain exaggeration would most likely be found in
   a. legends +
   b. memoirs
   c. historical fiction
   d. autobiographies
   e. essays

8. A scenario is
   a. a working script that contains dialogue +
   b. a transcript of an interview
   c. a script that contains dialect
   d. a character study within a written script
   e. all of the above

9. Which of the following five words is not related to synopsis?
   a. summary
   b. condensation
   c. brief
   d. abridgement
   e. documentation +

10. What genre is most likely to have its origins in folklore?
    a. fantasy stories
    b. myths +
    c. parodies
    d. historical fiction
    e. fairy tales

Sample Test Questions for the Storyscaping Exercises

Greater Difficulty

11. An apple pie is to an apple as
    a. a play is to a scenario +
    b. an actor is to a play
    c. a scene is to a setting
    d. a hero is to a villain
    e. a caption is to a cartoon

12. In a story, a resolution is to conflict as
    a. a question is to a problem
    b. an answer is to a question.
    c. a problem is to a solution
    d. a solution is to a problem +
    e. an answer is to a question

13. Which *two* of the following genres could be classified as either fiction or nonfiction?
    a. chronicle +
    b. memoir
    c. legend
    d. folk tale
    e. autobiography
    f. short story
    g. myth
    h. mystery +

14. Look for genre clues in this paragraph:
    After having assembled the time-machine rotunda, locate part **y** from the package box marked *Dangerous*! Carefully place part **y** in chamber 1, inside the rotunda. Push the red command button. Do *not* push the green ignition button. Congratulations, you just have completed phase four of the assembly process.

    Select *two* genres associated with the paragraph.
a. tall tale	e. adventure
b. technical writing +	f. reportage
c. stream of consciousness	g. satire +
d. transcript	h. advertisement

GA1506

Sample Test Questions for the Storyscaping Exercises

Greater Difficulty

15. Determine the genre from the provided story segments. Write the genre on the lines provided.

Lisa, perched atop her father's shoulders, could see the tall, gaunt and whiskered man on the platform. She had stood for hours, bored from the lengthy speech of the previous speaker. Even though she knew this was a speical occasion, she wanted this speech to be brief. She listened intently for the first few words. And they came in a high-pitched voice hardly audible to those assembled, "Four score and seven years ago . . . ." Her wish was fulfilled; the speech was brief.

_____
Historical Fiction

16. The apprentice gave the good knight his lance. The knight, on his mount, prepared himself with a silent prayer and primed himself for what had to be done. The grotesque creature bellowed flames from its evil nostrils. Slamming its tail upon the ground, a tremendous sound of thunder came. The knight, lifting his lance to an attack position, began the charge.

_____
Gothic Story

17. The first warm days of spring called us, like a siren, to the woods. There, above a carpeted floor of wood violets, we climbed trees and imagined ourselves to be Robin's band of merry men. The violets now are gone forever and the trees have been replaced with planted ones in tidy rows. The carpeted floor of spring purple has been re-carpeted with mowed grass upon which houses stand in their tidy rows. Robin, I wish you were back with your merry men!

_____
Memoir or Autobiography (Accept either one.)

Sample Test Questions for the Storyscaping Exercises

Greater Difficulty

18. "Blazing Trails" is a Western about rustlers and cattle barons. Don Autry, a retired marshall, is hired by ranchers to thwart rampaging cattle thieves. A deadly shoot-out occurs at the Red Butte Corral. Sheila Rogers and Bud Cassidy costar. A two-star motion picture. ★ ★

_____
Synopsis

19. Helen grabbed for the rope, but her frozen fingers made the attempt futile. How would anyone find her in this crevice? *Warm the hands*, she thought! *Warm the hands!* She attacked her backpack ferociously, stuffing the combustible things in her pocket. She found the matches! She held them close to her. *At least a chance*, she thought.

_____
Adventure

Match each definition with the correct word. Write the correct letters on the lines provided. No definition will be used more than once. Some definitions should not be used.

Words			Definitions
20. Dialect	____	(i)	a. language in subtitles or words accompanying a cartoon
21. Jargon	____	(f)	b. recorded conversation
22. Transcript	____	(b)	c. persuasive language
23. Caption	____	(a)	d. interactive language between actors in a play
24. Satire	____	(g)	e. language spoken by actors in a play
25. Ads	____	(c)	f. technical language
26. Monologue	____	(l)	g. humorous language that mocks or pokes fun at things
27. Script	____	(d)	h. a summary
28. Dialogue	____	(e)	i. regional language
29. Parody	____	(j)	j. mimicking a writing style or story
			k. written recollections
			l. a speech
			m. conflicts within a story

Comments and Acknowledgements

This author generally renews himself every five years or so. The renewal involves going back into a classroom for a year, which I did in Guilford County, North Carolina, during the 1991-1992 school year. I did this to validate my work; get euphoric once again about kids; and to trade hugs, lumps, and witticism with teachers. And perhaps in the most strange and mystical way, it rekindled and built a tremendous desire on my part to write something different. This is why I must acknowledge so many people because so many of them were within me when I began to think about this book and when I finally sat down to do it.

Also included in this acknowledgements section are teachers from Arizona who were a part of a three-year Javits Grant project entitled *Getting Gifted*, under the direction of Dr. Stephen Lapan, Center for Excellence in Education, Northern Arizona University, Flagstaff. I spent several days there for three consecutive summers. They, too, stimulated my mind and energy to do this book.

The North Carolina List

Bill Farkas	Paula Johnson	Ann Raker	Julie Bowlin
Judy Dockery	Betti Lowe	Carole Rankin	John Frey
Jean Bills	Linda Meyer	Alecia Walker	Erin Graham
Lori Casazza	Susan Middleton	Lynda Williams	Eric Hendren
Katherine Gilbert	Denise Pegram	Amada Wilson	Sam Kelleher
Jane Nelson	Janet Royster	Mary Wingard	Jolie Nance
Susan Norris	Vickie Royster	Lauren Yodis	Andrew Pate
Marilyn Schultz	Sheena Slade	Roxane Lehmann	Lindsay Peeden
Jacqueline Bailey	Annette Shuping	Denton Lehmann	Jason Schneider
Nancy Baker	Kim Stanley	Ben Tennant	Scott Turner
Jan Citron	Kay Bailey	Megan Davis	Sarah Bucior
Gail Lung	Mae Rodgers	Lauren Clarke	Melissa Godwin
Frances Paschal	James Harding	Stephanie Feltis	Kierston Mason
Anne Fleming	Myra Aderholdt	Ben Lambeth	Kevin Smith
Jane Hahn	Nancy Barrett	Lindsey Dominey	Jared Wilson
B.J. Hicks	Carolyn Brown	Kevin McGhee	Jordan Wolff
Rosemarie Mallard	Carolyn Burke	Adam Paisley	Kristy Jackson
Carol Newton	Sue Causey	Adam Fresesman	Carrie Kington
Anne Clendon	Cheryl Clifton	Kyle Downs	Steven Orndorff
Cynthia David	Margie Collins	Ashley Shaver	Jason Smith
Mary McDonald	Ellen Curtis	Brent Weatherman	Jessica Yanusz
Margeret Van Poucke	Diane Dillon	Amber Brown	Keith Bolte
Judy Wray	Nicki Hicks	Kate Brandon	Sarah Yanusz
Camilla Lewellyn	Pearl Hicks	Tommy Orndorff	Scotti Wilborne
Kathy Wrenn	Lenora Hill	Evan Turner	Alexander Vos
Cynthia Brown	Cristy Joyce	David Wooten	Jason Rogers
Cindy Dixon	Brenda Laferriere	Christopher Buck	Roxanne Leggett
Mary Todd	Helen Ledford	Cory Peters	Laura Kern
Cindy Bryne	Ann Lewis	Jonathan Miller	Robbie Gossett
Leisa Harrell	Allison Blough	Judy Williams	Trudi McDonald
Peggy Doss	Lynne Moody	Jewell Hammock	David Muir
Kerry Harris	Cheryl Pace	Becky Booth	Karla Partin
Kelli Clark	Patty Potts	Nicole Hoffman	Tommy Powers
	Karen Holt	Judy Provo	

GA1506

Comments and Acknowledgements

The Arizona List

Fannie Lomax	Mary Ann Harris	Rebecca Mc Carty	Lilly Curley
Linda Austgen	Vince Averett	Marsha Siglin	William Siglin
David Baxter	Faith Lutz	Zilm Synda	Thomas Sibcy
Kathie Sweet	Randall Sullivan	Cecilia Gowan	Mercy Spence
Venita Yazzie	Janie Colter	Zelma King	Marie Vasquez
Richard Sweet	Irene Tsosie	Sylvia Griego	Scott Anderson
Roberta Tayah	Jill Evans	Gwen Williams	Nancy Brown
Kim Tuttle-Truijillo	Nancy Jennings	Amajean Whitehair	JoAnn Erwin
Susan Lingle-Bartley	Joan Thompson	Elsie Uentillie	Margaret Roth
Judith Hart	Mary Ann Chee	Anna Nerini	Delores Lopez
Shirley Smith	Thomas Rago	Stephen Wheeler	Brenda Ault
Marilyn Tso	Madeline Becker	Roxanne Luna	Matt Kraemer
Patti Fisher	Arny Leslie	Paul Carlson	Audrey Young
Pauline Carbajal	Diane Laguna	Suzanne Kisselberg	Joy Hiebert
Patricia Rosas	Nattie Bedonie	Robert Becker	Rossaline Tahy

Students in a doctoral program at Northern Arizona University
who were involved in the "Getting Gifted" Project

Bob Sam	Kathy Tucker	Jim Granada	Cheryl Jackson
Pat Tejada	Bill Gibson	Rebecca Stump	

Special mention to . . .

Bill Farkas, Summerfield, NC, a principal whose school was a joy to be in and behold.

Roxanne Lehmann, Greensboro, NC, a talented parent of talented children, who is the epitome of parenting and volunteering.

Mary Henri Fisher, Greensboro, NC, a best friend, administrator, coordinator, innovator and a wonderfully irreverent person, who told me I would have fun in Guilford County. I did!

Stephan Lapan, professor, Center for Excellence in Education, Northern Arizona University, Flagstaff, for being a long-term resource, innovator, wit and visionary whose efforts have made a difference for many gifted minority children.

Zelma King and Cecilia Gowan of the Navajo Nation, Kayenta, AZ, whose minds carry the serenity of meaningful thoughts. I have learned much from them.

Sam Sanders, a craftsman and entrepreneur-of-sorts in Benton, IL, who remodeled a house and installed an office where I could think, write and snooze.

Troy Cole, Edwardsville, IL, a colleague, best friend, writer, consultant and cofounder of S & C Associates for his timely terrestrial and extraterrestrial thoughts and assistance on the manuscript and other matters.

GA1506

References

Amabile, Teresa M. *Growing Up Creative*. New York: Crown Publishers, Inc., 1989.

Booth, David W. and Stanley Skinner. *ABC's of Creating Writing*. Toronto: Globe/Modern Curriculum Press, 1981.

Loughmiller, Campbell and Lynn Loughmiller. *Big Thicket*. Austin: University of Texas Press, 1985.

McLuhan, T.C. *Touch the Earth*. New York: Simon & Schuster, Inc., 1971.

Stanish, Bob. *The Ambidextrous Mind Book*. Carthage, IL: Good Apple, Inc., 1990.

Stanish, Bob. *Creative Approaches to Teaching (Book 2): A Classroom Journal for Writing, Pasting, Drawing, Webbing and Coloring Things*. Buffalo, NY: D.O.K. Publishers, 1990.

Stanish, Bob. *Lessons from the Hearthstone Traveler*. Carthage, IL: Good Apple, Inc., 1988.

Stanish, Bob. *Mindglow*. Carthage, IL: Good Apple, Inc., 1986.

The Da Vinci Resources

Berenson, Bernard. *The Italian Painters of the Renaissance*. London: The Phaidon Press, Ltd., 1967.

Clark, Kenneth. *Leonardo da Vinci*. London: Penquin Books, 1978.

The Istituo Geografico De Agostini S.P.A. *Leonardo da Vinci*. New York: Reynal & Company, 1956.

McLanathan, Richard. *Images of the Universe. Da Vinci: The Artist as Scientist*. Garden City, NY: Doubleday, 1966.

Zubov, V.P. *Leonardo da Vinci*. Cambridge, MA: Harvard University Press, 1968.

Recommended Readings
Whole-Mind Approaches for Teachers
of Young Elementary Grade Students

Cole, Troy W. *Figure 8 Animals: Creative Ideas Across the Curriculum*. Carthage, IL: Good Apple, 1993.

Cole, Troy W. *Minding Minutes with Minute Minders*. Carthage, IL: Good Apple, 1994.

Stanish, Bob. *I Still Believe in Unicorns*. Carthage, IL: Good Apple, 1992.

Wayman, Joe. *Let's Talk About It!* Carthage, IL: Good Apple, Inc., 1986.

Beautiful Stories

Clement, Claude. *The Painter and the Wild Swans*. New York: Dial Books, 1986.

Paterson, Katherine. *Bridge to Terabithia*. New York: Avon Books, 1979.

Saint-Exupery, Antoine de. *The Little Prince*. New York: Harcourt, Brace & World, 1943.

Tomkins, Jasper. *Nimby*. San Diego: Green Tiger Press, 1982.

Beautiful Insights

Franck, Frederick. *The Zen of Seeing*. New York: Vintage Books, 1973.

Harjo, Joy and Stephen Strom. *Secrets from the Center of the World*. Tucson: The University of Arizona Press, 1989.

Lankford, George E., ed. *Native American Legends*. Little Rock, AK: August House, Inc., 1987.

McLuhan, T.C. *Touch the Earth*. New York: Simon & Schuster, Inc., 1971.

Summer Rain, Mary. *Whispered Wisdom*. Norfolk, VA: Hampton Roads Publishing Company, 1992.